MY BLACK FRIDAY

How I died twice to find HOPE

SHAWN C KELLY

MY BLACK FRIDAY

---

www.myblackfridaybook.com

ISBN: 0615689558
ISBN-13: 978-0615689555

Printed in USA

DEDICATION

To my beautiful wife Stacey, without whom this book would have never been written. Thank you for the words of inspiration, love, encouragement and always believing in me. You are my soul mate, my partner and the only one I want to share Jesus' name with all over this world for the rest of our lives. I love you so much.

CONTENTS

	Introduction	Pg vii
1.	My "Sweet" Sixteen	Pg 1
2.	Where Do I Belong?	Pg 15
3.	Is This Where I Belong?	Pg 29
4.	My Death	Pg 39
5.	Left For Dead	Pg 51
6.	My Awakening	Pg 61
7.	Baby Steps	Pg 81
8.	How Did I Get Here?	Pg 97
9.	The Next Step	Pg 121
10.	Learning to Love	Pg 135
11.	Testing Your Faith	Pg 147
12.	Do Something That Scares You	Pg 155
13.	Hope	Pg 171
14.	The Next Chapter	Pg 183
15.	Second Chances	Pg 201
	Afterward	Pg 213
	Letters From Friends	Pg 215
	A Letter To My Soul Mate	Pg 235

ACKNOWLEDGMENTS

This book would've never been written if it was not for everybody listed below. The book was written with love and I would like to give a special thanks to all of them:

- My children - Tana, Tyler, Jordan & Jacob
- Jessica Kubik
- David Kubik
- Mike Windeknecht
- Rich Rang
- Gerald Evans
- Selina De Rose-Juarez
- Bill Jameson
- Brandy Edwards
- Bob Lind
- Nicole Willin
- Stacy Dorsey
- Clarence White
- Bob Bell
- My Hope Family

A special thank you to my graphics and editing team, David & Jessica Kubik.

(949) 735-6709

info@kubikdigital.com

www.KubikDigital.com

INTRODUCTION

ANEW & CHILDLIKE

While writing this book, I have spent hundreds of hours searching and seeking to find the right words to convey my story and the message that you or someone you know may benefit from reading. I've even spent weeks secluded at the beach and mountains while I receive inspiration from God. You'll find as you read my book that I mention God and His words from the Bible. That is because I believe that the Bible was not given to increase our knowledge, but to change our lives. My life was changed for the better and it is because of how I have applied the Bible verses in my life.

My story, as well as so many other people's, tells a message of hope; a hope through Jesus Christ alone. While reflecting on my life, my circumstances and my choices, I completely have experienced a peace that passes all understanding, which can only be from God (Philippians 4:7). As I sit by the ocean and marvel at its beauty and creation I am confident that we are all made for a purpose. We are not created to wander a life, lost for numerous reasons, some by our own choices and/or things that have happened to us. We are created to live a life far better than you can imagine (John 10:10). We were made and thought of by our God who thinks the world of us.

I have a question...Why me? What makes me so special that I have decided to write a book? I am a professional addict. I know how to manipulate people to get what I want. I know how to deceive others in thinking that I'm normal. I have much experience with hiding anything I don't want anyone to know. I can justify any terrible behavior. If I stole from you, you wouldn't even realize it and probably would've done the same to me. If I hurt your feelings, well you're just too sensitive. If I lashed out irrationally at you, I was teaching you a lesson.

My past behavior can be summed up in this passage: My name is Shawn and I am an alcoholic. This is what addicts do. You cannot and will not change my behavior. You cannot make me treat you any better, let alone with any respect. All I care about, all I think about is my needs and how to go about fulfilling them. You are a tool to me. Something to use. When I say I love you I am lying through my teeth because it is impossible for someone who is an active addict. I wouldn't be drinking if I loved myself. Since I don't, I cannot love you. My feelings are so pushed down and numbed by my alcohol that I could be considered a sociopath. I have no empathy for you or anyone else. It doesn't faze me that I leave you hungry, lie to you, cheat and steal from you. My behavior will not change and cannot change until I make a decision to stop drinking and follow it up with a plan of action. And until I make that decision I will continue to hurt you over and over again. Stop being surprised. I am an addict and this is what addicts do.

This makes me sound like a horrible person,

but it's the truth. These are the traits that make addicts successful in getting what they want for a long period, without being found out. I used to be able to convince anyone to give me money for what they thought was going towards bills, but instead I was using it to buy alcohol. I used to look people straight in the eye and lie so convincingly that they thought I was a whole different person. I was a "functioning addict" which means I was able to keep my job, relationships and possessions all while being addicted to alcohol. This eventually caught up with me, but I was able to function for much of my twenties and thirties.

So again I come back to the same questions: why me? With all the mistakes of my past, why should I be writing a book? These questions race through my head all the time, and sometimes my self-doubt gets in the way, but I know it shouldn't, because I have faith that it's God's story that I'm writing and not my story. I believe we are a product of our past but we don't have to be prisoners of it.1.

---

[1] Rick Warren

The Bible says in Romans 8:28, "And we know that God causes everything to work together for the good of those who love God and are called according to His purpose for them." He chose to use me to write an incredible story in my life, and has given me the authority to share it with everybody I can.

God has given everyone a story. Maybe it isn't a life or death, earth-shattering story, but it is *your* story. God tells us to share it with others so it can encourage or inspire others to know that they are not alone. Whether we have had a "normal" life or one of dysfunction, pain or hurt, God can turn it to good. Once we release it, we can fully know what it means to go forward, release the past and live a new life with no regrets. I live with no regrets of my past because I am continuing to learn about me, who I want to be and how God sees me.

When I start questioning myself again I am reminded of a great song by Casting Crowns called, "Who am I." The lyrics say,

But maybe you still think not you, not because of who I am, but because of what You've done, not because of what I've done, but because of who You are. Lord, you catch me when I'm falling and you've told me who I am. I am yours, I am yours.

It is not because of what I've done in my life that makes my story worth sharing; it is what God has done.

God has given me hope and purpose in my life. He has given me the task of telling everyone what He has and is doing for me and for you. I'm speaking for Christ Jesus Himself now.

CHAPTER 1

"SWEET" SIXTEEN

"You can be in the storm, but don't let the storm get in you."

- Joel Osteen

Who am I? This question haunted me my whole life. When I was a kid I attended a private school where I was taught about Jesus. I thought I had an understanding about what Christianity was all about. I believed in God and heaven and even went through confirmation as a child, but I didn't know any more than that. As I entered high school, I slowly stopped following Christ and having a relationship with Him. Then as I became an adult, I almost completely forgot about Jesus. He had become a childhood memory of what things used to be, and over time I lost my purpose, meaning and direction in life.

Going back to my childhood, I remember being scared a lot. I have many memories of not wanting to get out of bed in the middle of the night because I was terrified. I remember many nights I wet the bed because I was too afraid to get up and go to the bathroom.

From the outside it looked as though my family life was the normal, typical family, but that wasn't the case. I have a brother named Jason who is a couple years younger than me, and an even younger brother named Aaron. Aaron and I have a thirteen-year difference in age and weren't very close as kids. By the time I was in high school he was right at the age where he was beginning to talk. That was fun for me because I had a lot of words I wanted to teach him. I would invite my friends over and encourage them to ask him to say cuss words. And he did! Some of Aaron's first words he ever spoke were bad words.

Growing up Jason and I were close but also very different. I was sensitive and always worried about what other people thought of me, yet I was popular and very good in sports. I always wanted everybody to like me. My brother was the complete opposite; he really didn't care if people liked him or not. He was always getting himself into trouble. I remember hearing a knock on at the door one evening when I was about eight years old. I followed my mom to the door and as it opened we saw a very angry woman with a distraught daughter standing next to her. I remember looking at the little girl and her hair looked as though it should've been in pigtails. Apparently it had been in pigtails, but my brother decided to cut them off. So there was the angry mom standing in front of my mom with her daughter's pigtails, one in each hand.

Another time, I must've been around the same age, my dad cashed a check and had given the money to my mother. It was a Saturday morning and I was watching cartoons. Jason wasn't with me, he was out looking for trouble. He eventually found the money in my mom's wallet. He took around $200 and ran outside after hearing music that makes every kid scream out, "Ice cream man!" But that's not what Jason screamed. He ran out of the house yelling, "I'm gonna buy the ice cream truck!"

He didn't buy the truck, but he did buy every kid on the block ice cream.

He wasn't sensitive like me and never really worried about what others thought about him. Sometimes, I wished I could be more like him.

My dad had a very tough exterior. He worked in the oil fields for over 20 years and was in and out of prison for various reasons my whole life. People saw him as very tough, a little crazy, and very intimidating. I liked telling people my dad had been in jail, but looking back now I believe it's because I was always looking for approval from everybody, especially my dad. Maybe it was because I wanted to be tougher than I actually was, and I thought if people knew how tough my father was then maybe no one would mess with me.

Growing up the only father I had ever known was always working, locked up or never home. Maybe that's why I never felt safe or possibly because my dad wasn't home to protect us. I remember one night when I was little I woke up to the police at our house. It was late and very dark. I shuffled outside in my pajamas and saw police taking photographs of our garage. It had been completely smashed in. I later learned that a drunk driver ran into our garage and fled the scene with his car. In my mind, I thought it was intentional and that he would come back to hurt us. He never did, but the idea that he knew where we lived stayed with me for a long time.

I also remember another time the fence on the side of our house was spray painted with the word, "THIEF." This also terrified me. I thought the people who wrote that might come back to harm us too. A good dad should be a protector and shield his family from these kinds of situations. My dad did the opposite. Years later, I found out the graffiti was done because of my dad; he had been caught breaking into a neighbor's house. They retaliated with vandalism.

Even though my dad continually disappointed me, I still sought his approval and wanted him to be proud of me. In my mind that meant I had to be the best in everything. I was gifted with talents allowing me to be good in all sports. Because I wanted to please my father, I put a lot of pressure on myself.

My mom and dad were polar opposites. She was always very loving to my brothers and me. She drove us to soccer, baseball, football, BMX racing, basketball, and pretty much any other sport you can think of. She would do anything for us. She was also very good at hiding things, especially from my dad. Every time we went clothes shopping, my brothers and I knew our job was to remove the tags from the clothes so my dad wouldn't see the prices. That way my mom could hide the actual amount of what she spent.

She had me at a very young age so she wasn't able to finish traditional high school. Instead, she worked hard to get her high school diploma and slowly chipped away at getting a college degree. She eventually finished school with her Masters in Education. I remember she was always very nurturing and tried hard to shield my brother and me from some of the things my dad was up to, but of course, she couldn't hide it all.

On my 16th birthday, I broke the school record in cross-country running. This was a significant achievement for me, because I was only a sophomore and the former record holder had been a senior.

I planned to get my driver's license that same day, but instead I was on restriction and had to wait a few more days. The day finally came to get my license. I remember being at a friend's house when my mom called me home, telling me she wanted to take me out to lunch before getting my license. I was excited; In my mind, I thought I was getting a car. On my "sweet" sixteen I got the shock of my life. My mother had no choice but to tell me that I had a different last name. She knew that I would see it on my birth certificate and could no longer shield me from the hurt it might cause. I found out the dad who raised me my whole life wasn't my biological father. She told me my biological father left me when I was only a couple months old.

My family rarely talked about this after it finally came out. When I tried to talk to my mom about it she would start to cry. My dad refused to discuss it with me, and I did not want to upset him, so I never pressed the issue with him. So, for the next 12 years we never spoke a word about it. As much as I didn't like my dad growing up he still is my dad and I love him. He raised me and loved me the best way he knew how.

Every child seeks to be like his family members in some way. I always saw how different I was from Jason and wanted to be more like him in some areas. I also acknowledged how different my dad and I were, which I was thankful for. But on that day, I finally understood why I was so different from both of them. This started to create a deep void within me. I knew I was missing something in my life, I just didn't know what it could be.

The year after I found out my dad wasn't my biological father, the pressure I put on myself to please him was lifted off my shoulders and I began hanging out with a different crowd. I found myself ditching school a lot, drinking and going to parties. I eventually quit running and gave up on all of my dreams of becoming a professional athlete. I walked away from several scholarships to college and a future I thought I wanted. I found myself drinking a lot and becoming depressed. I even started smoking cigarettes. I tried almost everything to fill the void within me and to find where I truly belonged. How could this all happen to me? I was a track star! How could I do all these things to my body and future?

I didn't feel the need to impress my dad anymore so I didn't continue to pursue the areas in my life that I was using to try and make him proud of me. I no longer felt driven to succeed nor did I desire to fulfill my dreams. At that time in my life, I didn't care. I had no worries except where the next party was going to be.

CHAPTER 2

WHERE DO I BELONG ?

"The easiest thing in the world to be is you. The most difficult thing to be is what other people want you to be."

- Leo Buscaglia

After high school I still had the nagging desire to fill my deep void. I continued battling depression and loneliness. I had no idea what I wanted to do with my life. I felt like an 18-year old loser with no purpose. Because I had abandoned my dreams, I was left with no goals or ambition.

I met a girl whom I thought would fill the empty space in my heart. I decided getting married was the next step I should take in my life. All throughout high school there was always some confusion about which last name I should be using. My wife decided she wanted me to stick with my "real" last name, which I shared with my biological father. I didn't feel comfortable changing it, but I wanted to make her happy.

After a month of marriage, we felt it would be a brilliant idea to have a baby. At the time I was working about 8 hours a week, making minimum wage at a job I had no future in.

This wasn't working. I found a new job at a drug store. I started at the bottom and knew if I worked hard enough, I could advance to the top and eventually make some very good money. As I worked my way up the ladder I thought I found my purpose again. I felt good about myself and I was happy. I thought my job was the key to what I felt was missing my whole life. I was wrong.

After a long, hard day at work I constantly came home to a sleeping wife and daughter. Night after night I found myself not ready for bed yet, so I would turn on the TV and accompany myself with two beers. Soon two beers turned into four. Then four turned into six. I continued this pattern for about 6 years, working hard during the day and spending my evenings with my liquid companion.

By this time I was drinking around a 12-pack of beer every day, which did not go unnoticed by my wife and mom. They repeatedly told me that my drinking was out of control, and after some time I decided to quit drinking. I became a "dry drunk."

When I was a dry drunk I was no better and no worse than when I was still drinking. I was addicted. I had poured all my attention into beer. After I quit drinking, I became addicted to my work. I was constantly looking for the next dollar, the next promotion. I wanted something to replace the alcohol I thought I was missing. To be honest all the things I tried to replace the alcohol with were only temporary. I needed something, anything that would fill the big giant hole I felt deep within me.

Over the years I couldn't stop thinking about my biological father. At the age of 28, I wanted to know more about him. Knowing he existed somewhere left me with a lot of questions, the biggest one being: how could a father leave his son and never desire to have any form of communication with him? I had recently found out my wife was pregnant and we were going to have a boy. I started thinking more about what a father/son relationship looked like. I wondered what he looked like. Do I have any brothers or sisters? He could've found me easily; why didn't he? Was he even alive anymore? I thought if I had answers to these questions I would finally feel complete.

One day I got the nerve to look for him, but I didn't know where to begin. The only information I had about him was his name and birthday. I called some private investigators, but it turned out I didn't have enough money to compensate them for their time. Everyone who knew about this quest kept asking me: Do you have his social security number? I didn't have it. I thought I hit a dead end. Something inside of me wasn't ready to give up yet. One afternoon I found myself at the Social Security Office. I had no idea what I was doing there because I didn't have his social security number. I walked in, stepped up to the first window and explained my situation to the woman behind the desk. While I was talking she began typing. When I quit talking she stated, "Here he is." She said it so plainly, so simply.

My heart dropped. In the blink of an eye she found my father.

I didn't know what to do. I was speechless. The woman went on to explain that I could write him a letter and they would mail it for me. She said they weren't allowed to give out his address, and it was up to him if he wanted to respond.

I left the social security office numb. I didn't know what to say or do. I entered the building anticipating that they would tell me I was out of luck, my father was nowhere to be found. Now I had to think about what I was going to say to this man. How do you write a letter to a stranger that you know is going to completely change both of your lives?

It took a few days before the numbness wore off, and I wrote the letter. I don't remember much about the content of the letter, but I do remember that I made it perfectly clear that I didn't want any money from him; all I wanted was to meet him. I sealed up the letter and had the Social

Security office mail it for me. Now the anticipation began.

Only a week had gone by, when I checked the mailbox and there it was! A letter addressed to me from a person with my last name! I was a little confused and in a fog. I opened the letter and, sure enough, it was my real father. How totally insane. He wrote back saying that he lived in New Mexico, but he was a truck driver and was driving through California in the next couple days. He wanted to know if he could stop by and meet me. I said yes and we made plans to see each other.

Waiting for his arrival felt like the longest days of my life. So many thoughts went through my mind. Why did he leave? What did he look like? Do I have any brothers or sisters? I convinced myself that I would be happy if I could meet him just one time and that I didn't want anything from him. However, deep down inside I hoped for something more.

At the same time, I was trying to decide if I should tell my dad. We never had an open communication where we talked about serious topics, especially when it came to strong emotions. So I decided to only tell my mom.

Well, the day finally came and went. I saw what my biological father looked like for the first time. I looked just like him! It was totally crazy looking at him; our hands looked exactly alike. We looked so much alike it was scary.

I knew growing up that my mother was only 16 years old when she had me. What I didn't know was why he left. During our brief time we spent together he never answered those questions for me. He tried to convince me that he didn't know about me. I knew this was a lie because my mom told me that he was at the hospital when I was born and signed my birth certificate. I was hurt once again by him, but I pushed the feelings away before I could let his lies get to me. Months passed before I ended up seeing him one more time. This time I found out I had two more brothers and a sister. He also told me that my sister was graduating high school so I decided to drive out to his place to meet them in person. It was so awesome to see my sister and little brother. I found out the other brother, who was a little younger than me, was nowhere to be found. He didn't want anything to do with our biological father. When I asked my father about it he wasn't honest with me and brushed over it. To this day I have never met my other brother and don't know where he is. I think about him a lot because I feel the pain he must be going through. I hope and pray I get the opportunity to meet him one day.

While I was visiting with my new family members there were some people who approached us saying that there was no mistaking us for father and son. If they only really knew what I was struggling with internally. The truth was my biological father had known about me and abandoned me, whereas everyone else believed he had no idea I existed. It really bothered me when people commented on how much we looked alike. I wished I could have told them that not only did we look alike, but we had a lot in common, but I couldn't. He had never given me the opportunity to know him. The only significant knowledge I had of this man was that we have the same DNA. These comments were just another reminder of the disappointment and rejection that was so hard for me to deal with.

I realize that even to this day I am always looking for approval and acceptance. When I look back on my relationship with my dad and biological father I wanted them to accept me and love me. I felt like I was either too sensitive, or not enough. The way I viewed my father figures followed me into my adulthood. I was always looking for a new father figure, whether it was a boss, friend, or anybody who would love me and give me acceptance which I so desperately wanted. Yet again, none of these people filled that void.

CHAPTER 3

IS THIS WHERE I BELONG?

"You never can ever get enough of what you don't need to make you happy."

- Eric Hoffer

By the time I was 34 years old my marriage was over. We experienced two separations, and by the third time we were ready to call it quits.

My divorce left me with so much anger, and I didn't know how to deal with it. Soon I began showing signs of depression. I was satisfied with my decision to end the marriage since it wasn't a healthy relationship, but I struggled with feeling like I had taken a giant leap backward.

Even though I had negative feelings about my divorce, there was a part of me that was relieved. I experienced freedom that I hadn't felt since I was a teenager. I hadn't had a drink in 10 years. I convinced myself that because I had gone such a long time without alcohol, I clearly didn't have a problem and I could control it.

I still worked hard, pouring more hours into my job than I should have and making a decent living for myself. After a hard day's work I rewarded myself by going to the same bar every night and getting wasted.

It was the combination of my new-found freedom and anger towards my ex-wife that led me to drinking again. It got bad very quickly within weeks, and worse than it had ever been. I used to only drink beer, but this time I went straight to hard alcohol.

Following the divorce I moved in with my mom. She allowed me to stay in her small, extra bedroom where I slept on a twin bed with furniture that didn't match. In the den was a computer I would use to look up old friends on Facebook. I spent a lot of time reliving my glory days by friending people from high school who remembered me as the popular athlete I used to be. They had no idea that I was living with my mommy and battling addiction. I was able to use Facebook to escape my reality and pretend like I was in high school again.

Around this same time I ventured out, began to meet new people and dated and dated, and dated some more. I frequented strip clubs a couple times a week, all while drinking myself into a stupor.

One day I decided to buy a new car. I thought I deserved a new car. When I was married I chose to drive our older vehicle because I wanted my wife and kids to be safe in the newer one. Now that I didn't have to drive the junky one I wanted to make up for the times I had to park on a hill backwards so I could push the car in order to get it started. So without any hesitation I bought myself a Mercedes. Of course, later that night I celebrated my new purchase, picked up my little brother and went to a bar. I had a few drinks, met some "ladies" and we all decided to go bar hopping. After three bars (or so) we knew it was time for us to head home. I got on the freeway, looked at my brother and said, "Let's see how fast this thing can go." As I began testing the limits of my new car I sped all the way up to 139 miles per hour. We would've gone faster had the governor's chip allowed. I lost control and miraculously stopped within inches of crashing into a tree. My brother and I were stunned. He looked at me and in a drunken haze screamed, "RUN! RUN!" I wasn't going to leave my new car, so I tried starting the engine. Before I knew it, we were surrounded by cops and I was arrested for DUI.

After spending a night in jail, I was finally able to make my one phone call. I didn't have access to my cell phone so I had to come up with the numbers from memory. I racked my brain trying to think of phone numbers, but I was only able to think of one. After much hesitation I finally picked up the pay phone and dialed my daughter's number.

I had hurt so many people around me; even my mom was at her wits' end. I was oblivious to the stress, pain and heartache I had caused her, as well as my other family members. Unfortunately, at this time, I was so out of control that I didn't care about what happened to me. That was all I knew because I hadn't really grown as a person or matured as an adult. However, this was still not enough to get my attention. If I were a cat, I think I already used my nine lives. I was living life as an addict, believing I was indestructible, and not caring what damage I left behind in my path. All I cared about was myself. What's amazing is that God could have easily said, "It is over; that's enough!" But, even though I was clueless, lost and searching, I believe He had His hand on me all along.

CHAPTER 4

MY DEATH

NOVEMBER 26, 2006

"Doing more of what doesn't work won't make it any better."

- Unknown

My "Black Friday" began probably just like yours. It was the day after Thanksgiving, but I didn't go shopping. Black Friday, for me, was always the busiest shopping day, the beginning of Christmas season, and I did not look forward to it. I had spent the last twenty years in retail management, so this day meant preparing all the sale items weeks prior, getting up extremely early, handling all the crowds and, not to mention, the angry customers if we ran out of merchandise. I thought I was prepared for this "Black Friday," but little did I know, this one would be very different.

Early that morning began when my alarm went off at 2:30 am. I got up and started my day just like any other day. I was the first to arrive in the morning around 3:30. On the way to work I wasn't feeling my best, but I thought it was because I was awake so early and stayed up late drinking the night before. Soon after I arrived, a couple of other employees arrived and we began to hang all the advertisement signs for the sale that was going to begin. I remember only half of the store lights were on because it was so early that the timers hadn't turned on the other set. As I was hanging signs I started feeling worse than when I woke up. My stomach felt like I had a big gas bubble and then I became really nauseated and found myself in the bathroom throwing up over and over. I couldn't stop and I didn't want to leave the bathroom in case I had to throw up again. I began to sweat like crazy and my clothes were drenched.   Finally after vomiting for what seemed like thirty times, I made it out of the bathroom and went to my office. I was sitting at my desk, pale white and dripping with sweat when my secretary came in. I said something to her I have never spoken in my life. I told her, "Take me to the emergency room!"

As my secretary drove me to the hospital, I couldn't talk. I was in intense pain and I started to cry. We arrived at the hospital and the nurse took one look at me, handed me some paperwork and told me to have a seat. I guess from my age of 35 and weighing only 155 pounds she wasn't too concerned about me. The pain I was in continued to worsen, and I was crying even more. That's when my secretary yelled to the nurse and demanded they take me back and have a doctor look at me. I still had no idea what was going on and neither did anybody else. They no sooner got me into a bed, when I had two cardiac arrests. Both of these cardiac arrests flat-lined me and they had to perform CPR and shocked me back to life.

I remember opening my eyes to see several doctors and nurses huddled around me. I wasn't sure what was going on, but my chest and ribs really hurt. I found out later that during CPR a doctor had broken one of my ribs. I looked around to see nurses crying. Someone informed me of what had just happened and said, "You are very blessed to be alive."

From that moment my life changed forever, but not in the way you might think. I was only 35 years old; how can this be happening to me? I felt so scared, terrified and depressed. Who was going to take care of my kids if I didn't get better? Why me? All of these questions started racing through my head and at that very second I felt so alone.

This "Black Friday" was the day I questioned who I really was. Things changed, I was no longer a husband, a dad, a jock, popular, sober or healthy. What now? What do I do? Who am I? I was mentally and physically broken.   No longer did I have the titles that I had worked so hard to have. Now, the only title I thought I had was "heart attack victim", but I survived.

I am a statistic. I am a miracle. Less than 5% of people survive a cardiac arrest, and I suffered two cardiac arrests, and one heart attack in the same day. Currently over 20% of my heart is damaged. I will always have to take 5 or 6 medications a day and I never go anywhere without carrying a vial of nitroglycerin in my pocket.

You would have thought that my "Black Friday" would have been my rock bottom, my wake up call. It should've been the pivotal moment in my life that made me realize how badly I was hurting myself. Unfortunately, it wasn't. I still didn't get it. I continued to spiral, making bad choices, while running from truths. Instead of having an attitude of gratefulness for being alive, I became more self-destructive. I didn't care what happened to me. I had died twice already and wasn't afraid to die again. I was depressed, angry and empty.

For the next two years following my "Black Friday" my drinking got more out of control and I started combining alcohol with prescription painkillers. My health continued to decline. My blood pressure and cholesterol were extremely high and I gained around fifty pounds. To top it off I had the beginning stages of cirrhosis of the liver. Needless to say I was on a path to death.

I was so depressed and lonely that I was looking to alcohol, drugs and women to fill the big hole in my heart. I eventually lost my manager position and filled my days drinking from the time I woke up until I passed out. I did this every day while taking about thirty painkillers. I went to dentists and doctors to get my fix. I even resorted to sneaking and taking them from my mom. I also stole them from my brother and when he found out about it, he secretly switched his pills with a laxative and I spent two days in the restroom. When my brother didn't have what I needed I stole some from my daughter after she had her wisdom teeth removed. I needed something more in my life; the alcohol and drugs weren't enough.

I didn't know it at the time, but what I really needed was to work on myself. Over the years I lost who "Shawn" was.   My kids were exposed to stuff not even adults should experience. My daughter, who was 18 at the time, had to pick me up from jail or the hospital on more than one occasion. She saw me night after night drinking myself to death, so did my son. I thought he was too young to know anything, but I couldn't have been more wrong. I was constantly looking to get into fights, getting kicked out of bars; my friends even called my mom to tell her that I was out of control.

At this point I was like a violent tornado, ripping my life apart. A twister doesn't care what's in its path and neither did I. All that mattered to me was finding a way to get myself to an altered state so I didn't have to deal with my reality. This method of living was working for a while and I thought I could continue living this way without anybody stopping me. I was wrong.

CHAPTER 5

LEFT FOR DEAD

"You can't rob God and expect Him to bless you at the same time."

- Joel Osteen

One day I came in contact with my first love from high school. She was the first serious girlfriend I ever had. She was older and a beauty queen. She broke my heart back then when she cheated on me and I had difficulty trusting women from that point on. Even though I knew our history, I still didn't care. I needed to fill the fast-growing empty hole I had in my heart with something; and at the time I thought she would be the answer.

I should have known it wasn't good from the start. She was going through a bad divorce. Over the next several months I pushed her and her kids on my kids. I put her before my children and their feelings. She became my drinking partner, so my relationship with her got worse and worse. By the end of our relationship, I was having a lot of problems with her and her kids.

Things came to a head, and worsened one evening when she didn't come over to my house after she said she would. I decided to get hammered and drive drunk to her house, which was forty-five minutes away.   Thank God I didn't kill anybody driving over there. Apparently I didn't learn from my DUI.

I arrived at her home and passed out, parked in the street for two hours with my car still running. When I came to I walked up to her front door and her ex-husband answered. He told me that she didn't want to see me anymore. I said some choice words to him, turned around to walk to my car and was struck from behind. The next thing I remember was waking up in the ER. I had suffered a severe concussion, bruising behind my ear, lacerations, black eyes, neck and back pain and a chipped front tooth. Luckily, a neighbor had seen what happened and called 911. If that wasn't bad enough I had to call my daughter (again) to come pick me up. She should have never seen me in that state.

The guy who beat me up was arrested for assault with a deadly weapon and booked into jail. He was bailed out later that evening and given a court date. I was determined to be in that courtroom when he was arraigned.

I wanted to hurt the man who hurt me so bad. It would have been so easy to do this myself or have it done. During the time I wanted revenge on him, I found out where he lived, worked and what type of car he drove. I found myself watching him and driving by his house. I'll be honest and tell you at the time I didn't know why I didn't do it. I struggled with this for quite some time.

When the court date of his arraignment finally came, I showed up and so did he. The case was called and postponed. The District Attorney wanted more information and sent the report back to the police department. I was outraged. He was out of jail and nothing was going to happen to him.

Over the next few months and then years I called the police department and the District Attorney's office attempting to get information. I hated the way they made me feel. I felt like I was the defendant; I was the victim. I wanted justice for what he had done to me! Then one day when I called the police department they couldn't find the report and told me the District Attorney must have it. I called the D.A. and they told me that the police department had it. This went on until finally the case ran out of time. The statute of limitations was up, and the case was dismissed. I didn't understand how this could be happening.

The following weeks I thought hard about my life and the choices I'd been making. I wanted to stop drinking. I actually wanted to live, but I didn't know how. I needed help, but had no idea where to go. I didn't have health insurance anymore. I couldn't check myself into rehab. I had no idea what to do. Every recovery center I called was $20,000, $30,000 or even $40,000. I couldn't believe it. How can anyone afford those prices? I told one recovery center if I had that much money I would still be drinking and doing drugs. I even found some free programs, but they had very long waiting lists. They were also one- to two-year programs. How can I leave my kids that long? How can I change on my own? Everyone in my life was just about done with me. I burned so many people and bridges. I knew no one was going to loan me that much money. I didn't feel like I had any options. I became more depressed and lonely.

Looking back, the funny thing about the man who hurt me was that I wasn't sure if I should remain hating him or thanking him, because if this beating had never taken place I wouldn't be here today. I'm sure I would be dead. When you really think of it, this guy saved my life by beating me almost to death. I'm not sure if I would ever thank him, but I forgave him.

It's ironic that I wanted revenge and suffering for this man. I was so outraged that he felt it was okay to hurt me; meanwhile I was doing a pretty good job of killing myself on my own! Funny, how we harm ourselves repeatedly by our lifestyles and choices but don't want to take responsibility. However, if someone does us wrong, we want "justice." Good thing God doesn't give us what we deserve. He gives us chance after chance by giving us grace.

CHAPTER 6

MY AWAKENING

"Therefore, if anyone is in Christ, he is a new creation; old things have passed away; behold all things have become new."

2 Corinthians 5:17

Many have asked me what my rock bottom was. When did I finally get it? How did I get sober and turn my life around? Was it after my cardiac arrests? Was it after hearing I had cirrhosis of the liver? Was it after I was beaten up? I can't point to one exact moment; I believe it was all of those things combined. These events had to happen to me so God could get my attention. I was so lost in my addiction and sin, I had to lose everything in order to gain everything.

There were several times after my "Black Friday" that I wanted to be healthy and sober, but had no idea how to get there. Everybody thought they knew what I needed and were constantly telling me what to do. I ignored everybody no matter if it was my best friend, family or my kids. How and why won't I listen? Am I not ready? Do I even love my kids, family or my friends enough to make a change?

One evening my mom told me about a little church down the road from where we were living. She talked highly about the church and the pastor. She asked me to go and check it out, and maybe meet with the pastor for counseling. I reluctantly agreed and went to the service. When I arrived I was greeted by some very friendly people. The church service was really nice and made me feel safe enough to make an appointment with the pastor for counseling. I planned to meet him the following week on a Tuesday at his office. Tuesday approached and, of course, I couldn't go all day without drinking. So, I drank before the meeting. I brushed my teeth and popped some breath mints hoping this would help the smell. While waiting in the office I started making up reasons why I already didn't like the pastor. When I walked into his office I noticed it was a mess and nothing matched. Again, I started to judge. We began conversing and after a lot of meaningless talk he saw right through me. He was very straight-to-the-point and I didn't like it. After the appointment I left and never went back. I looked for every excuse NOT to listen to this man and he knew it. I made a lot of prejudgments, but the truth was I didn't like hearing the truth. I needed to change, but I found it was easier to look at others, judge them and point out their faults and problems.

After the experience with the pastor, my mom was at her wits' end and thankfully still wanted to help me. She asked me to contact my uncle, "the preacher man". I called him just to appease her, and he asked me to come over to talk. I had the same frame of mind during my last preacher visit so I was convinced this "holier than thou" man who had never done anything wrong, and whom I barely knew, couldn't tell me anything I needed or wanted to hear. However, I still agreed to meet with him. Deep down I knew I needed to change. I was still looking to fill the void I had felt for so many years. Did my uncle know the answer? There was a small part of me that was open to hearing what he wanted to share with me. I popped some pills, filled my bottle full of Vodka and drove 50 miles to see him.

This Christian, "goody two shoes" man, whom I always thought was perfect told me his good, bad and ugly life story. He shared experiences from his life and problems he dealt with in the past which I related to. He was the first person to open my eyes to the possibility that I wasn't alone after all. I saw how my uncle had overcome so much from his past. It made me think I might one day have success like he had.

At the end of our time together my uncle asked me if I wanted to accept Jesus into my life. I wasn't sure exactly what this meant, but I knew my uncle held the key to what I'd been searching for so long. I agreed to accept Jesus and was overwhelmed with hopefulness. I began to cry as my uncle prayed for me (James 5:16). He invited me to attend church the following Sunday and I agreed to go. I stepped one foot out the door and left his house feeling the nag of my addiction.

When I got into my car to drive home I started to drink again; I didn't even wait until I got home. What is wrong with me?

That following Sunday I showed up at church. I didn't really want to be there but I knew if I didn't show up on my own, my uncle would have driven to my house to pick me up and I would be there anyway. I did my same routine of trying to sabotage these opportunities to change and I purposely didn't shave my face. I also chose what I thought was an inappropriate outfit: shorts, a t-shirt and a baseball hat. I was looking for anybody to say something to me; I wanted a reason not to come back. I even wore my hat during service.

No one said a word to me about my dress attire or hat, and I was really surprised. The worship band began to play and they were amazing. I started to become less critical and really connected with the guy singing. He was a little younger than me and looked pretty cool, but the way he sang was like nothing I had ever experienced. The way he worshiped God was so powerful. The tears I saw running down his face was something I wanted, but I didn't cry. Why can't I get this "Jesus thing?"

The service ended and I remember standing outside the church talking with my uncle. The worship leader came and introduced himself to me as Bryon. I talked with him for a couple minutes and could tell he was a good guy. The following Sunday I went back to the same church, wearing the same outfit as the previous week. I still hoped to myself that someone would say something negative to me. Again, no one did and as my uncle and I approached the entrance, the worship pastor, Bryon, said to me, "Hi Shawn." Out of all the people in this huge church, he remembered my name. This gave me a small glimmer of hope and acceptance that I desperately needed and wanted. From that day on I was sold on this church and began making some significant changes.

I continued going to church over the next few weeks and began experiencing a relationship with Jesus. I had another new friendship that began to matter even more than alcohol. Any time I spent at church gave me happiness that I hadn't experienced since I was a kid.

I stopped drinking, but continued taking a lot of narcotic pain pills. I still popped between 10-15 Norcos a day, which was down from the 20-30 I had previously been taking. Even though I shouldn't have been taking any pills at all, change was beginning to happen.

During this time, I struggled with a feeling that haunted me, and ultimately started my path of hopelessness. I thought the choices I made in the past would stay with me forever. I always believed I would spend the rest of my life paying for the poor decisions I had been making. In my hopelessness I was trapped in a downward spiral that I couldn't seem to get out of. The more time I spent getting to know God, the more I was able to climb my way out of this trap I thought I was stuck in. My turning point was realizing God sent his Son, Jesus to take the punishment I deserved for the choices I made (John 3:16). I don't deserve what He did for me. No one does. Everyone sins and we all deserve to spend eternity in Hell, but that is why Jesus died on a cross (Romans 3:23). We can spend eternity in Heaven with Him, instead of getting what we deserve by accepting Him as our Savior and living a life that is pleasing to Him. We don't have to be haunted by our sin.

God gave me a fresh start, a new beginning. He wiped my sin-filled slate clean. I was beginning to find even more value in having Jesus as part of my life.

I continued building my relationship with Jesus which involved reading my Bible every day. I came across a verse that changed my way of thinking forever. The verse reads "...Christ Jesus came into the world to save sinners—and I am the worst of them all. But God had mercy on me so that Christ Jesus could use me as a prime example of his great patience with even the worst sinners. Then others will realize that they, too, can believe in him and receive eternal life." I Timothy 1:15-16. It was a pivotal moment in my life where I was able to make sense of how much my new friend Jesus really loved me. I related to Christ in the same way I related to my uncle. This verse helped me realize Jesus understood what I was going through too and that everyone needs what Jesus did on the cross. No one needs the cross more; we all need it differently.

When growing up, I had a best friend, Chris. We met in 4th grade, and did everything together. We had the kind of relationship that some people never get to experience. We shared everything including our toys, clothes, even our girlfriends. We were inseparable; if I wasn't at his house, he was at mine. There was no knocking on the front door; it was understood that we always had permission to enter each others' homes. We were like family, even closer.

Eventually that slowly changed. We went to different high schools and tried to stay in touch, but we both started to meet different people and before I knew it, we weren't communicating as often. We began hanging out in different cities with different people. Our friendship, which at one time was unbreakable, was hardly a friendship anymore. It got to the point where we would go months without talking to or seeing each other. Eventually those months turned into years.

When I look back on my time as a child I think of the relationship I had with God. I used to spend much time reading about Him and talking to Him every day. I used to think about Him all the time, but just like the relationship I had with Chris, my relationship with God slowly faded away because I stopped investing time in Him. I still went to church once in a while, but the only communication I had was when I needed something from God. It's not like I stopped believing in God. Just like my relationship with Chris, we grew apart, but it didn't mean I still didn't love and care for him.

Someone can say they are a Christian their whole life and truly believe Jesus is their Savior, but what happens when they stop talking with Jesus or following Him? My life personally fell apart. I slowly found myself so far away from Jesus I could hardly hear Him anymore. I was living with my eyes fixed on nothing but my own desires, and over time my life slowly unraveled.

God wants to be the ultimate friend. Friends run to the phone to call one another when something good or bad is happening. God wants to be the one we call for everything. You can't call someone your "best friend," and never talk to each other. You have to invest in the friendship. God wants you to share the good, the bad and the ugly. The Bible tells us, if we call on Him, He will be there for us (Jeremiah 29:12).

Another way I like to think of it is if you want to date someone. You plan to hang out and get to know each other and spend quality time together. The more time spent with one another, the more the relationship grows. I am thankful for my friendship with Chris and thankful for our relationship through the years. However, I am even more grateful for my friendship and relationship with God.

During the time I was strengthening my relationship with Jesus I began viewing this friendship as a father/son relationship. I had experience in my life with a father whose approval I desperately needed. Never pleasing him scarred me emotionally. Through building my relationship with Christ, I found that Jesus was the ultimate, perfect father, and therein began a desire to please Him instead of my dad. The more time I spent knowing God, the more I learned about His desires for me. I also learned that God has a plan for my life that involves my utmost dreams (Jeremiah 29:11). I found purpose in my life; in no way did alcohol or drug use fit in that picture. I used to wake up every morning, reaching for the bottle, looking for my first high of the day to take me away from reality. It was why I got up in the morning. Then my focus shifted and it was my new-found purpose which was driving me to get out of bed and continued throughout the entire day. At the end of the day, my purpose in life outweighed my desire to use.

Have you ever heard someone say, "It will take an act of God to..." That's exactly what happened to me. It literally took an act of God to change me. I didn't go to rehab, and only attended a couple AA meetings. After four months of going to church, I was clean and sober. My life changed tremendously in those few months. I poured every ounce of my being back in to church. I began replacing old habits with newer, healthier ones. I never felt obligated to be there because I knew where I would be without God. I knew that Jesus Christ was my Savior. He forgave me. He died on the cross for my sins, and I realized how much He loved me. I had been so lost without Him. I tried filling the huge void in my heart with alcohol, drugs, material possessions and women. None of it worked.

All the months and years I spent searching and looking for my purpose, it was right in front of me. The Bible says, "Train a child up in the way he should go, and when he is old he will not turn from it." Proverbs 22:6

Like I mentioned before, I went to a private school when I was young. I knew Jesus Christ and had a relationship with Him. My mom did an amazing thing by putting my brother and me in private school to learn about God and get the best education we could get. We were given the foundation and were trained up in the way of God. I believe that deep down feeling I was having most of my life was worsened when I walked away from the Lord and tried living my life on my own terms. That feeling I had deep down that something was missing was the Holy Spirit. It was everything I was taught as a kid growing up about God.

The huge void in my heart was created by God to be filled only by God. Another way to put it is: The only One who can truly satisfy the human heart is the One who made it (Acts 17:24-27). As life happened, the hole in my heart grew and grew into an oddly shaped puzzle piece that I tried hard to fill with the wrong pieces. Jesus was the only puzzle piece that fit perfectly in that spot.

My life was finally headed in the right direction. In no way was I cured of my addictive nature; I will always be an addict. But I no longer felt that I was in a battle by myself. I had God on my side, fighting with me and for me. The same

God who conquered death was on my team, and it is a battle I will have to fight every day for the rest of my life.

CHAPTER 7

BABY STEPS

"The steps of a good man are led by the Lord. And He is happy in his way."

Psalm 37:23

I **remember shortly** after I found God again and falling in love with Him all over again, I was painting my mom's house to earn some money. I had just dropped my son off at school, and was heading over to her house to get some more work done. I remember how beautiful that day was outside and I was driving really slow enjoying the beautiful weather. I was so lost in enjoying my surroundings I almost didn't realize I was getting pulled over by a police officer. The officer walked up to the window and asked for my driver's license, registration and insurance. I gave him my registration and insurance and told him I must have forgotten my license at home. He immediately asked me if I even had one. I responded yes. As soon as I said it, I knew I was wrong. My license was suspended because of my drunk driving. The officer went to his car and called in everything. He came back and told me to get out of the car. I immediately put my hands behind my back and told him I totally understood that he needed to arrest me. I also said I was sorry for lying to him about having a license. The police officer asked me why I didn't tell him the truth. I explained I really didn't know, I was sorry, and he could arrest me. He told me if I had just been honest from the beginning the situation would have been different. He went on to explain that because he had called it in, his boss overheard everything, and there was nothing he could do about it. I agreed and told him again to do what he had to do. He told me he wasn't going to arrest me, but he was going to impound my car for 30 days. I told him I understood; he was just doing his job, and I shouldn't have been driving on a suspended license. He proceeded to tell me the only reason I was pulled over was because I was going too slow. This was so ironic because I usually drive too fast! He also told me I was a very nice guy and felt bad for doing this to me. The police officer let me get everything out of my car I wanted and he even let me call for a ride. What an awesome officer. While we were waiting for the tow truck he told me to have a seat in the back seat of his car. I remember sitting back there and telling God how sorry I was. I told him that I would serve Him for the rest of my life. That was the day I said goodbye to my Mercedes. I never picked it up from the impound yard. I was finally figuring out where I was going and who I would follow.

In 2 Corinthians 5:17 it says, "Therefore, if anyone is in Christ, the new creation has come. The old is gone, the new is here." I was ready to be a new creation, free from the mistakes I'd made and ready to make better choices in my life.

I started constantly watching Christian TV and listening to Christian music to fill my day and attended as many church groups that were available to me. Instead of trying to get that next "high" on alcohol, I was getting "high" on God. He was the answer and I couldn't get enough.

I was finally at a time in my life where I was able to make a full, complete commitment to God. It didn't happen overnight. I'd heard many addicts say to me, "One day at a time." I later found it in the Bible. Matthew 6:34 says, "So don't worry about tomorrow, for tomorrow will bring its own worries. Today's trouble is enough for today."

But even thinking one day at a time was too much for me. It began with small steps that eventually led me to the end of my destructive road, onto a new path that was totally dependent on God. One of the first steps I took was scheduling a specific time during the day to pray to God. I spent a lot of time asking God to help me with various areas in my life, especially with honesty since that was a big struggle for me at the time. I also thanked God for giving me a second chance, waking me up, my health, and my kids. I remember feeling like I had another chance to make the same choices over again, and I prayed that God would help me make the right choice and I could make good on the second chance He had given me. Soon I was praying two, and then three times a day.

Another step I took towards recovery was journaling. This was a new habit that I put into action. My journals aren't the typical journal where someone chronicles the events that unfold in their life; instead, my journals include interesting quotes I found, my response to them, and some snippets of information about my day, as well as my thoughts and feelings. I took my journal with me everywhere; I still do this today. Over time I found that when I wrote down my thoughts, prayers, and steps I had taken so far, I was able to look back and to see how far I had come. I can laugh at some things I was thinking, struggling with and praying about that seemed so huge at the time and reflect on how petty and small they were. It is amazing to read about situations and circumstances and realize how God worked them out.

At the same time I was creating new habits, I began to slowly replace my old habits. I used to cuss quite a bit and I remember thinking to myself that there's no way I can stop all at once. It had become part of my vocabulary and I depended on these words to get my feelings across. So instead of eliminating these vulgar words I began limiting the number I would speak. My bad words went from 15 a day, to 14, down to 13, and so on until I had eliminated them completely.

One of my favorite sayings is "Fake it till you make it." In other words the more I practiced being positive in my thoughts, words and actions the easier it got and the better I got at it. Even if I wasn't happy at the moment, I acted like I was and later I would find out I wasn't just acting or faking it. It had become a reality. I don't encourage you to be something you aren't, I am encouraging you to be more positive and good things will follow.

The changes I was making weren't always received so easily by some of the people I hurt in my past. I remember a few old employees had confronted me and asked why I never apologized for things I had done to them, said to them, or how I treated them. I had to be honest. At that time, I wasn't sorry at all. I had to learn to forgive myself first, I wanted them to know I had really changed; that it wasn't just words. Change was happening and sometimes I didn't even realize how much. I had made a commitment, to myself, to be transparent and genuine to people. I had fooled myself and others for so long that I wanted to be real and live with no more regrets.

Another baby step I took was running the Facebook account for the church. I was in charge of putting a positive quote online each day, building the friend list, posting pictures and keeping the members informed of events.

Because I wasn't drinking or using anymore, I had a lot of time on my hands. I began spending six days a week at church, and I lived 45 minutes away. I completely submerged myself in a lot of different areas. I worried less about me and more about pleasing God. I actually was given an award at church for being so dedicated in serving, they even provided me with a sleeping bag and a pillow. I tell people today that going to church and serving saved my life because it is what has kept me centered.

Opportunities for me to grow in my faith and as a person were happening daily. I once heard someone say, "Whatever you are looking for; you will find it." If you are looking for trouble, you will find it. If you are looking for excuses, you will find them. If you are looking for truths and opportunities and seeking God's will, you will find those too (Proverbs 23:7).

The biggest commitment I made to God was when I decided to get baptized. Christians view baptism as a public expression of an inward change. When a Christian is baptized, he/she enters into a covenant with God, agreeing to follow Him for the rest of their life. Baptism embodies much more than this, but I like to think of it as a couple who decides to get married. They stand in front of their loved ones and make a public confession that they vow to be true to one another until the day they die. When I was baptized, I made a promise to God that He would be put first in my life.

On Father's Day of 2009 I was baptized by my uncle. It was an amazing experience for me. I sat in what felt like a gigantic bathtub, and an overwhelming feeling of guilt washed over me. I couldn't stop thinking about all the horrible choices I'd made. My uncle, standing outside the tub, grabbed both of my shoulders and dunked me completely under. I remember coming up out of the water feeling clean inside. It was almost like God pressed a "do over" button inside me. Getting out of the water felt like I left all my sin in the tub and was finally free of anything and everything that could ever hold me back from the life God wanted for me.

It was roughly three months before my baptism when I stopped abusing painkillers. This would technically be called my "sobriety date." I don't have any special kind of chip to commemorate this day, nor do I even like calling it a "sobriety date." I remember going to one of the few AA meetings I've ever been to, listening to a man share his story about how he was 19 (or so) years sober. While I recognize this to be a great achievement, I couldn't help but place doubt upon my own ability to stay sober for that long.

Many addicts have a hard time giving up their drug of choice because they have depended on their drug to help them through something they feel they can't get through on their own, and often view it as a friendship they're not ready to let go of. I struggled with this for a while too. Even though alcohol got me into a lot of trouble, it was always there for me to transport me away from the reality of failing to feel complete.

I realized that I wasn't able to focus on my future because I was facing the wrong direction: the past. Once I shifted my focus away from my addictions and looked Heavenward, I stopped viewing the alcohol as a trusted companion. I never mourned the loss of the old friend I had in my addictions. Instead I celebrated the new friendship I had in Jesus Christ and looked forward to everything He has planned for me.

I like to think of my life and the choices I made as a fragile tree. I used to be planted in a garden that was full of weeds. The fruit I produced was ugly and inedible. My roots were so deep in this garden that eventually the weeds choked me to the point of near-death. God has uprooted me and I am in a new garden, planted in fresh soil. I am watered daily and the sun beams down on me. Now I produce fruit that is healthy and beautiful. This analogy of my life transformation comes from this verse in Colossians 2:6-7, "And now, just as you accepted Christ Jesus as your Lord, you must continue to follow him. Let your roots grow down into him, and let your lives be built on him. Then your faith will grow strong in the truth you were taught, and you will overflow with thankfulness."

CHAPTER 8

HOW DID I GET HERE?

'KIDS CAMP'

"The soul is healed by being with children."

- Fyodor Dostoyevsky

One Sunday after church, I came out to see my mom talking with the children's pastor. I walked over to them and, not wanting to interrupt, waited patiently for their conversation to end. As I stood there waiting, I heard my name thrown around a couple of times along with the words "Kids Camp." I was able to piece together that my mom had planned the next week for my son and me. We were going to Kids Camp.

As a teenager, I'd spent a couple summers as a camp counselor. At first I thought I would have something to offer and be able to teach the kids a thing or two. My feelings quickly changed and, getting on the bus, I was scared out of my mind. I felt like a little kid going away for the first time without mommy and daddy. I was only four months sober, and a beginner Christian but I jumped on the bus and up the mountain we went.

The first night the camp leader told us counselors our job was to pray out loud for each child in our group. He told us that most of the kids were homesick and needed prayer. I thought, "Who's going to pray for me?!?" I didn't have a lot of experience praying out loud, and I was able to get through it. In fact, it was through the feeling of fear that I felt proud of myself for being vulnerable and allowing myself to do something that scared me.

Over the next couple days I experienced more amazing things on that mountain. I met incredible people and was able to see first-hand what true faith looked like. I remember watching the kids and seeing how they worshipped during Chapel service. Those kids had it and all I knew was that I wanted it too. As the kids were experiencing the love of God, it brought me back to my first visit to church, watching Bryon lead worship and wanting so badly to be able to experience that kind of worship. I was finally able to let go of everything that was holding me back and began singing just like the kids. The tears finally came out. The hurt and the fears I felt couldn't be kept in any longer. Growing up, I always had to be tough and be strong but now I didn't have to prove anything to anyone. The feeling that came over me was something I never experienced before. It wasn't a bad feeling or a sad feeling, it was the best feeling I have ever felt. I loved it. I felt safe, loved and at home; I hadn't experienced this in a long time. I was being transformed into the person God wanted me to be.

I thought being a camp counselor was going to allow me to teach the kids and change their lives; however, they ministered to me. God had to take me away from everything and everyone, and put me on that mountain so I could hear what He wanted to tell me. He wanted me to come to Him as a child and learn to love Him as only a child can do.

I was reminded of an old song, "Go Tell It on the Mountain." This would become my mantra.

After I came down from the mountain I wanted to tell everyone what Jesus Christ had done, starting with me. I had a story to tell, and I wanted everyone to hear it.

"Go Tell It On The Mountain"

Go tell it on the mountain,
Over the hills and everywhere,
Go tell it on the mountain,
Our Jesus Christ is born

When I was a seeker
I sought both night and day,
I asked the Lord to help me,
And he showed me the way.

Go tell it on the mountain,
Over the hills and everywhere,
Go tell it on the mountain,
Our Jesus Christ is born.

He made me a watchman
Upon a city wall,
And if I am a Christian,
I am the least of all.

Go tell it on the mountain,
Over the hills and everywhere,
Go tell it on the mountain,
Our Jesus Christ is born.

Shortly after returning from Kids Camp, I wanted to do something big. God placed it in my heart to share my story with the church. The church I attended planned out their services a year in advance and our lead pastor didn't let just anybody speak at our church, especially not an alcoholic, drug addict, new believer. I didn't realize it at the time but God had his hand in orchestrating this and allowed it to happen in an extremely short time. My story/testimony was filmed by Bryon the worship leader and shown to 6 services and to over 3,000 people in just two weeks after coming home from Kids Camp.

I remember right before my testimony was shown I was praying to God that my story would touch just one person. I wanted to share how God could take all these terrible things I had done, things I had experienced, and turn them around. I was grateful for what God was doing in my life, and I wanted to share the hope I had found. After I was walking out of one of the services where my video was shown, I noticed a big burly guy standing outside. He approached me and I noticed he had tears in his eyes as he said, "You just told my story, thank you". This always reminds me of the saying, "Friendship is born at the moment when one person says to another, 'What! You too? I thought I was the only one.'"[2]

I was approached by several people in the following weeks. They shared with me that my story had encouraged them and given them hope. As I began to share my struggles and experiences with others, I was growing and deepening my love for God. I was motivated and there was no stopping me.

I didn't realize at the time that by sharing my story I had made myself very accountable. I had confessed my sins before thousands, and now there was no turning back. It wasn't like I could go into the store and buy booze and wonder if anyone recognized me. Looking back, this was another important step for me. Before, I didn't care who saw me and what they thought of me. There was no

---

[2] C.S. Lewis

more hiding my dirty little secrets, and I made myself transparent to those around me. I was moving forward, and there was no turning back for me. God was continuing to reveal things to me daily. As I drew closer to Him, and His will, He guided me to the next steps.

This is a newspaper clipping of my mom in front of our house after a hit and run collision. This picture was taken on May 5, 1975 when I was only 4 years old.

Oct 15, 1987 my sixteenth birthday, sophomore year. I set a new school record in Cross County at Etiwanda High School.

I was 19 years old. It was all business in the front and party in the back. (top)

My car I push started for two years. (bottom)

My son Tyler and I at the race track. He loved being on the motorcycle with me.

This was the first time meeting my biological father Garry. I was 28 years old.

This was the first time meeting my half brother Cody and half-sister Tenaya. I was 28 years old. (top)

This is me a month before having my heart attacks and two Cardiac Arrests. (bottom)

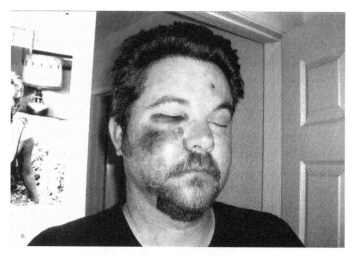

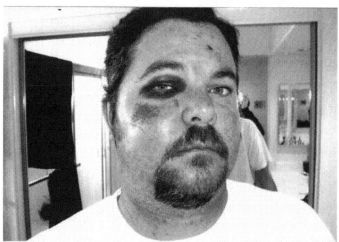

Photos after my beating.

My uncle the "Preacher Man" & my Aunt Wanda. (top)

This is the only dad I knew. He raised me from a couple months old. (bottom)

Vacation Bible School only a couple weeks after my testimony was shown to the whole church.

Here is the children's pastor who talked me in to going up to Kid's camp and later would become my mentor. (top)

My daughter Tana's High School graduation. From left to right - Myself, Tana, Tyler, Mom, niece Sidney, younger brother Aaron, brother Jason, niece Jasmine & niece Sam. (bottom)

Here's my new family. From left to right is my daughter Tana, son Tyler, wife Stacey, step-son Jacob, & step-son Jordan. (top)

Christmas 2011 - from left to right Jordan, Tyler, Tana, Jacob, Stacey & Myself. (bottom)

Grand Opening of Hope Recovery Center, Inc. on June 16, 2011. (top)

My beautiful wife, Stacey & I at Harvest Crusade in Anaheim, California. This photo was taken on August 25, 2012. (bottom)

CHAPTER 9

THE NEXT STEP

"I tell you the truth, unless you change and become like little children, you will never enter the Kingdom of Heaven."

Matthew 18:3 (NIV)

It was about two weeks after sharing my story that I was ready for a new challenge, something that was scary for me. I wanted to make a new commitment and I wanted that commitment to matter.

I read somewhere that we stop thinking like a child when we stop asking questions. Children do not know what cannot be done. I wanted to find a way to get back into that kind of thinking again. I signed up to be a leader for Vacation Bible School (VBS). I taught what I thought was the most challenging class: Bible stories. VBS was a five-day summer program where kids 5-12 years old could come, bring their friends and neighbors to experience Jesus in a fun way through music, games, crafts and Bible stories.

One of my biggest fears has always been public speaking. I remember hearing someone say once "Progress always involves risk; you can't steal second base and keep your foot on first."[3]   My biggest fear in life was starting to become my biggest passion! All I wanted to do was speak publicly and share what God is doing and how He can change lives if we allow Him to come into our lives by giving up control. In no way was I fit for teaching children. I began to learn that God does not call the equipped, he equips the called.

Vacation Bible School was amazing. I spent all night and most of the morning preparing for my lesson that I was going to share with the children. I learned so much that week and spent much time in prayer. By the end of Vacation Bible School I taught 6 times a day, for 5 days to children in kindergarten to sixth grade.

---

[3] Frederick Wilcox

I had faced my fear of speaking in public and God guided me through the entire process. That week changed my life more than I could imagine. After it was over my pastor asked me to come with him to open up a new church campus.

I agreed to go help the pastor, and dove into the children's department so quickly that I barely had time to think. I fell in love with those kids and fell in love even more with God. I couldn't get enough knowledge; I couldn't read or go to church enough. I read everything I could get my hands on and asked my pastor as many questions as I could. Before I knew it I was volunteering at the church six to seven days a week. As I was being "transformed" into a new person, I was growing so much. The kids asked so many questions, and I always had to be ready for the correct answer. I was being stretched more than I ever had been before. Not only would the children ask questions, but I found adults were seeking answers from me also. I was by no means an expert. Sometimes I doubted myself and thought, Don't they know who I used to be and where my life was headed a year ago? People saw my life changing and I wanted my actions to be real. I wasn't living a facade, I was living out true change from God and wanted others to see it too. People were seeing my changes from the inside out, and it gave me more opportunity to share my new-found faith and what God was doing in my life.

The children I taught were so honest and so full of faith. They helped me grow as a speaker. They provided feedback that no other adult ever could have. If they thought I stunk it up speaking, they let me know. When the kids were bored, they showed it. When they were interested in what I was saying, they were all ears. I never had to guess what they thought of me. They either loved me or hated me; their honestly always came through.

While listening to a Christian radio station one day, I heard this song for the first time and was moved beyond words. It is called, "From the Inside Out" by Hillsong United and it had a profound impact on me. It described everything I felt; like it was written about me. After hearing it, I played it over and over, taking in every word. To this day, it is my favorite worship song.

Hillsong United
"From The Inside Out" Lyrics

A thousand times I've failed
Still your mercy remains
And should I stumble again
Still I'm caught in your grace

Everlasting, Your light will shine when all else fades
Never ending, Your glory goes beyond all fame

My heart and my soul, I give You control
Consume me from the inside out Lord
Let justice and praise, become my embrace
To love You from the inside out

Your will above all else,
my purpose remains
The art of losing myself
in bringing you praise

Everlasting, Your light will shine when all else fades
Never ending, Your glory goes beyond all fame

My heart, my soul, Lord I give you control
Consume me from the inside out Lord
Let justice and praise become my embrace
To love You from the inside out

Everlasting, Your light will shine when all else fades
Never ending, Your glory goes beyond all fame

And the cry of my heart is to bring You praise
From the inside out, O my soul cries out

My Soul cries out to You
My Soul cries out to You
to You, to You

My heart, my soul, Lord I give you control
Consume me from the inside out Lord
Let justice and praise become my embrace
To love You from the inside out

Everlasting, Your light will shine when all else fades
Never ending, Your glory goes beyond all fame
And the cry of my heart is to bring You praise
From the inside out, O my soul cries out

Everlasting, Your light will shine when all else fades
Never ending, Your glory goes beyond all fame
And the cry of my heart is to bring You praise

From the inside out, O my soul cries out
From the inside out, O my soul cries out
From the inside out, O my soul cries out.

My favorite part of this song is the very first sentence, "A thousand times I've failed still your mercy remains and should I stumble again still I'm caught in your grace." I love these lyrics because I cannot fathom the idea that anyone would ever afford me mercy. I have done so much in my life not to deserve it, but something in me wanted to believe it.

I started craving growth and looking for more avenues to help keep me focused, and keep me positive. There are a lot of negative distractions around us in our lives including people, media, life and especially our thoughts. I found that reading a few quotes a day helped me keep on track. They were just quotes or verses that related to how I was feeling that day or where I was at, so I started posting them on my personal Facebook account and noticed I was getting good responses from other people. Then, I started texting people quotes for the day, and got even more positive feedback. It was exciting to find more people I could relate with. Funny how I had felt alone for so long, but actually there are so many people who feel the same way.

Some of these quotes were more than just words because I was putting them into practice, and into my belief system. It is one thing to know something, but it's far different to experience it and live it out. Before I knew it my Facebook grew from a couple hundred to several thousand people. Now I have close to 5,000 friends; I guess there are a lot more people out there who crave inspiring quotes.

It was around this same time that I had to attend my court-ordered classes for my DUI. I went once a week with about 35 other people who didn't want to be there. I remember hearing a lot of negative talk from some of the other class members, so I chose to stay away from them and spend my time close to the teacher who was actually interested in educating us on the effects of alcoholism. I remember we watched a video about intervention and it dawned on me to ask the teacher after class if it would be alright with him to share the video of my testimony I shared with my church. He agreed and the next week we watched it. I was a bit skeptical about how it would be perceived from my classmates, but to my surprise they were all very supportive and genuinely touched. They began asking me questions after class and seeking my counsel like I was some kind of expert. I know I wasn't an expert in overcoming addiction, but I did have some helpful answers. When I look back and evaluate my time there, I can't help but think maybe I was becoming to them what my uncle was for me: someone I could finally relate to.

I was on God's "fast track", and there was no looking back. In my opinion, I had been on the road to nowhere for so long, I had a lot of making up to do. God was stretching me, and taking me on an adventure. He was continuing to give me opportunities. I have always been the rebel doing whatever I wanted, asking for forgiveness later. In this new chapter of my life, I was actually allowing God to direct me, and I, for the first time, was walking in obedience and loving it. I was finally putting God first in my life.

CHAPTER 10

LEARNING TO LOVE

Life is about learning to love.

There is so much about my story that just doesn't make sense. For most addicts it's usually a similar story: addiction, rock bottom, rehab, AA, sponsor, recovery. This next chapter in my life (and book) was another detail that was out of the norm for someone going through recovery.

It was back when I was at Vacation Bible School where I first met Stacey. She was a children's leader just like me at Vacation Bible School. I remember thinking how cute she was. She was wearing a hat, capris and a fanny pack, where she kept all the kids' goodies, snacks, etc. I actually didn't meet her formerly until I gave one of my friends my written testimony to read on the last day of camp. Stacey was reading my testimony to herself when I noticed her approaching. She started reading over my friend's shoulder. It was then I was introduced to my future wife.

Two days later I saw her again at Harvest Crusades at Anaheim Stadium. I wanted to sit by her so bad, but my friend sat in between us all night. After the concert, as we were walking out I finally got an opportunity to speak with Stacey and ask for her phone number. We texted each other all the way home and well into the night. Within a couple of days we began dating. We shared our pasts, our backgrounds and our hearts.

The connection we had for each other was incredible. We both instantly fell in love and the rest is not history, because Stacey and I are not living in the past anymore. We are making our future. Though no one can go back and make a brand new start, anyone can start from now and make a brand new ending. Stacey and I married nine months later.

We wanted so many of the same things in our relationship, but there was one thing that stood out over the rest. We both wanted God first in our lives. We wanted to make sure the other knew that was a serious decision we each had made. I remember telling her that if she got in between God and me she would have to deal with my uncle Tommie. My uncle made sure she knew that the first time he met her, and he also fell instantly in love with Stacey. He told me right away after meeting her, "I like her. I like her a lot." When I heard those words come out of my uncle's mouth I knew she was sent from God. God knew He had to send a very strong woman of His to handle all of my mess.

God's ways are never early, but always on time (2 Peter 3:9). Ironically, Stacey had worked at the place where my grandpa had lived for a couple years and I had never seen her before Vacation Bible School. Although I had visited my grandpa several times before, our paths never crossed. Looking back, I was so lost and blind in my crazy life that I wouldn't have known how to have a good relationship with her. Although we probably had passed each other before, God had to open our minds and hearts and prepare us individually for us to come together. I believe God brings people into our lives and some things out of our lives in His time. I know Stacey had gone through her own struggles before I met her. I could say that I wished we had met sooner, but I know we both were so messed up in our past that it might not have worked out.

Over the next year I felt like God was preparing us for something so much bigger than we could ever imagine. After Stacey and I were married my son and I moved 40 miles to Corona, California to be with my new wife and her boys. Stacey in the meantime moved out of her home of nine years and we all moved in together, blending families.

We started a new ministry called Hope Recovery Small Group that met every Friday night. I became the director of the children's department at one of our extended church campuses. I talked Stacey into leaving the non-information-information booth (she called it that because she never had the correct information or knew what was going on) and come over to the children's department to help me run it. To top it off Stacey left her job of 8 years. Wow! What were we thinking? We weren't, we were being obedient and following God's direction for our life. We both so badly wanted a new life: a life where God was first in. We both knew that we had to stop questioning God and start trusting Him.

I have to be honest and let you in on a little secret. I don't know how to love. As an addict my one true love used to be alcohol and I would stop at nothing to protect our bond. Alcohol was always there for me, and I loved it for helping me escape so I didn't have to feel anything. It became my number one importance and I was devoted to it wholeheartedly. I know this kind of logic doesn't make sense to non-addicts, but we addicts have difficulty making sound, reasonable judgments because we live in a fog that is centered around our drug of choice. It's almost like I have a split personality. There's two Shawns: Addict Shawn and Real Shawn. Real Shawn struggles with pain, doesn't know how to deal with it and doesn't want to feel. Addict Shawn swoops in and finds ways of dealing with the pain no matter what the cost.

Once Addict Shawn takes over, it's difficult for Real Shawn to surface so Addict Shawn keeps on feeding the desire to use, all the while hurting everyone else around him. It's like the saying: "Man takes a drink and sooner or later the drink takes the man."

So like I said, I didn't know how to love another person...I didn't even know how to show love to myself. Even though this is something I am constantly working on, I believe we all don't know how to love. We've been given a perfect example of what love looks like in I Corinthians 13:4-7, "Love is patient and kind. Love is not jealous or boastful or proud or rude. It does not demand its own way. It is not irritable, and it keeps no record of being wronged. It does not rejoice about injustice but rejoices whenever the truth wins out. Love never gives up, never loses faith, is always hopeful, and endures through every circumstance." I only know of one person who can say they consistently show this kind of love, and that is Jesus Christ.

Without a doubt I love Stacey and she loves me. I believe the love God wants us to have is so much greater. He wants us living out I Corinthians 13:4-7 and having healthy, long-lasting relationships. God loves us so much that he sent his only son to die on the cross for our sins. I also believe that God sent His son down to Earth to be that perfect example of love. So we can have a perfect example of how to love (John 3:16).

The Apostle Paul tells us to look for good in all. Even when Paul was in the nastiest prisons we could ever imagine, he still gave praise to God and never lost his faith (2 Corinthians 12:9-10). Sometimes in marriage it's not always good, but we have to know that God will use those situations to teach us and grow us as Christians. I praise God for these teachings, even though they happen so much to me. I guess I have a lot of making up to do since I was so far away from God for so long.

My soul mate Stacey and I have so many differences. You might ask, doesn't that make things hard? Yes, but it is also amazing that God has given me so many different strengths than my beautiful wife Stacey. With Stacey's strengths and mine we are a force to be reckoned with. We are so powerful together. The Bible says in Ecclesiastes 4:12: "A person standing alone can be attacked and defeated, but two can stand back-to-back and conquer. Three are even better, for a triple-braided cord is not easily broken." I read a study once that if a man can lift 100 pounds, two men can lift 300 pounds. Wow! That doesn't even make sense to me, but to God it makes all the sense in the world. You see in Romans 12:5 it says: "so it is with Christ's body. We are many parts of one body, and we all belong to each other."

I fell in love with Stacey because I saw her heart and love for God. I know God put us together for a reason. God wants you and us to be in a personal relationship with Him and each other.

I thank the Lord every day for my soul mate and I thank Him for second chances.

CHAPTER 11

TESTING YOUR FAITH

"If God will bring you to it, He will bring you through it."

- Unknown

I **was finally** at a point in my life where I was on the right path. Even though I still struggled with my addictive tendencies, I never gave in to them. I was making more good choices in my life than bad ones. I was proud of myself.

I remember one afternoon I was visiting my uncle, excited to share with him how I'd been growing. My uncle was a wise, old man. Every time I got comfortable in my new way of living, he pushed me to the next level. While I was so excited to discuss all my accomplishments he stopped me and guided me to a verse in the Bible that says, "Consider it pure joy, my brothers and sisters, whenever you face trials of many kinds, because you know that the testing of your faith produces perseverance.   Let perseverance finish its work so that you may be mature and complete, not lacking anything." (James 1:2-4). This verse taught me that becoming a Christian doesn't mean my life will be free from hardships. In some ways, it's the opposite.

God tests our faith by stretching our spiritual maturity and Satan tempts us constantly. This is how we grow as Christians.   The more we are stretched by God and overcome temptation from Satan, the more growth takes place.

Here's another way to think of it: when you were in school the teacher couldn't take a test for you. It was the teacher's job to teach and was my job to learn. How does God teach us? Does He tempt us with something bad to see if we will do wrong (James 1:13)? I used to think He did, but I have learned from the Bible that God does not tempt.[4] Temptation comes from Satan and giving into temptation will only lead to sin. Satan is very

---

[4] Unknown

sneaky. He can even use beautiful things in your life to distract you from what God wants you to do.

God doesn't tempt. Instead, he tests us. What is the difference between temptation and testing? Temptation is designed to help establish a disobedience pattern in your life, but a test is designed to strengthen and mature you in your walk.

This is how I look at tests now. I look at Jesus as my teacher. He teaches me things and shows me the right stuff to be doing. After He teaches me, He will test me in order to show me where my strengths are and where my weaknesses are. The really awesome thing about our teacher, Jesus Christ, is He will tell you the answers and even give you a book with all the answers in it. He will let you retake the test as many times as you need and will let you take the test open book. If that still doesn't work He will send tutors in your life to help and guide you to the "A" He ultimately wants you to have. And all these tools are free of charge because Jesus Christ paid the price for us when he died on the cross. He took care of everything. The Bible even says in I Corinthians 10:13, "When you are tempted, He will also provide a way out so you can endure it."

It used to be that whenever I failed I would get very down on myself. Today when I mess up or things don't go my way, I ask God what He wants me to learn from this situation. Before I looked at failures as consequences; today, I see them as opportunities to improve, learn, and grow. Again, it is our choice how we see things. I am determined to pass the tests that I am given even if it takes me my whole life and 1,000 chances.

CHAPTER 12

DO SOMETHING THAT SCARES YOU

Courage is being scared to death,
but saddling up anyway.

I **once read** somewhere "Do something every day that scares you." This quote stayed with me for a long time. I accepted it as a personal challenge and began looking for ways in my life I could apply it. For me, this meant stepping out of my comfort zone on a daily basis.

As I've shared this quote with many people they've asked me, "Why would you want to do something that scares you?" My response is always the same. Doing something that scares me takes courage, and I am showing my faith each time I do this. I know that God is going to show up each and every time. It's difficult to think that way when you're scared, but that kind of mentality is what stretches your faith. If you don't have to stretch your faith maybe you don't need God. When you do stretch your faith, you put yourself in a position to be able to see God come through for you in ways you could have never imagined.

I like to think of it this way: if you exercise the same way every day, your body will get used to the workout and your muscles won't strengthen. You need to change it up so your muscles will grow. I want my knowledge and my faith to grow so I have to exercise those in the same way I would exercise my muscles.

I often tell people how big my God is. I know how great He is because I have proof in my life of how He can take the worst of sinners and make something good. I also challenge other Christians by asking them, "How big is your God?" Some Christians know how big God is, but haven't experienced it personally. I know my God is huge because I have tested what He will do for me. I have constantly put myself in scary situations and He provides what I need every time. He might not be early, but he's always on time. The more I test Him, the bigger my God is to me.

The best way I stepped out of my comfort zone was recognizing different areas of my life I needed to change. Why is change so hard? There is a story a friend told me a while back. It was so sad and yet so powerful because I believe it relates to me and maybe you.

There was an older married couple who had decided to adopt a baby. Although this sound likes a happy event, it was not so easy. They brought the infant home and were told of her difficult beginning. She had been extremely neglected at only a few months old and was rarely held or touched. When the new parents would go to take the baby out of the car seat, the baby would scream and cry without stopping until she was put back into the seat. Later they found out that the baby's body was actually conforming to the infant seat. Slowly and patiently the parents began holding the baby and touching the baby, but this was not an easy process. Over time the screaming of pain began to decrease.

As adults we are similar to that baby. We might have been in a bad situation as a result of something we have done or something that has happened to us. We don't want to change because of the fear of the unknown. We might even resist change because it is so uncomfortable and painful for a period, just like the baby. But the truth is we can change. We need to stay out of our comfort zone in order to change. Life is not always easy or fair, but God can and will work everything out for His purposes if we allow Him, and surrender all the bad that we have held on to for so long. We can choose to live in our dysfunction, circumstances and beliefs because it is all we know or we can try something different. The definition of insanity is doing the same thing over and over again and expecting different results. I got to a point in my life where I realized I was making so many wrong choices, and I wasn't getting the results I wanted so I changed radically and began making newer, better choices. God gave me courage to change into the man He wanted me to be.

I never knew the definition of the word courage until I looked it up one day and to my surprise it said, "the ability to do something that is scary." I had already been challenging myself by pushing past the fear and making the changes in my life I needed to make. The word courage is such a powerful word, and knowing I had such a word describing steps I was taking in my life propelled me and drove me forward even more.

There are so many ways that I demonstrated my new courage: speaking in public, writing things down and sharing my goals with others. Each time I did this I was stretching my faith, getting more "God muscles", holding myself accountable and allowing others to hold me accountable.

Now I have become a man who does what I say I am going to do. Of course I'm not perfect but I've learned that when you speak it out loud, and write it down, it becomes part of your belief system.

There is power in it. We all know that words can hurt us, many of us deal with scars from the past, and it keeps us from moving on to our future. Write down your positive thoughts, goals, and dreams. If it is difficult, start small. Tell it to someone or a group. Make a plan. You can't reach your destination if you don't know where you are going. God has given you a map and the tools to get through whatever comes at you in life. It is called the Bible (Basic Instructions Before Leaving Earth). It is not a fairy tale, and it isn't any less powerful today than when it was written. There is so much there that pertains to our lives, our desires, our feelings, and what we are going through. Look at different translations of the Bible, you may notice that the ones with footnotes are especially helpful so you can understand and learn and it will speak to you.

We don't have to let fear stop us from changing. I was able to push past the fear because I had faith that God would come through for me, and He always did. "Faith is being sure of what you hope for and certain of what you cannot see" (Hebrews 11:1).

Whenever someone asks me about faith, I refer them to Matthew 17:20 which says; "'You don't have enough faith,' Jesus told them. 'I tell you the truth, if you had faith even as small as a mustard seed, you could say to this mountain, 'Move from here to there,' and it would move. Nothing would be impossible.'" A mustard seed is one of the smallest seeds. It is about as big as the tip of a pencil. This is such an encouraging verse for me because Jesus is saying that even if we have a little bit of faith, it can be enough to move an entire mountain. Someone struggling with addiction doesn't have to have a huge amount of faith to make positive changes in their life; I sure didn't. It can all start with faith the size of a mustard seed. My small faith began with believing God can take the impossible and make it possible.

Once you do have a little bit of faith, it's important to build on that faith and allow it to grow. That means we need to get rid of the doubts that stop us from reaching our goals. In the past, I always used to think, what if something bad happens? Or what if I fail? Or even what if God doesn't come through for me? I had to change my thinking and stop doubting myself and, more importantly, doubting God. I began asking myself: What if good things happen? If we truly walked in faith and courage knowing that God is on our side, we don't have to be afraid of the "what ifs?"

So let's address the scary thought of: what if something bad happens? God never promised things would be easy and we wouldn't have any problems. Becoming a Christian doesn't conclude your life with good things happening all the time. It doesn't mean your life is going to be perfect.

It's like this: when a man joins a football team, he goes out onto the field expecting that someone is going to run into him and tackle him. He's dressed for it. He's prepared for it. He knows it's coming because that's all part of the game. In that same way, Christians know we're going to be faced with trials. We can anticipate tackling, and it's all part of God's plan. God isn't a masochist. He gives us these trials and promises He will turn our challenges into rewards, stepping stones for our promotion.

Earlier I mentioned the time my uncle Tommie pointed out the verse in James 1:2-4. I'm now able to look at it with a new perspective. It says, "Consider it pure joy, my brothers, whenever you face trials of many kinds, because you know that testing of your faith develops perseverance. Perseverance must finish its work so that you may be mature and complete, not lacking anything." James points out that we should be joyful when we are faced with difficulty because we have something to overcome which, hopefully, will make us a better person and draw us closer to God. I used to think that when bad things happened it was God punishing me for my poor choices. It's the exact opposite. God gives us opportunities to grow into mature Christians, not as a punishment, but because He loves us.

Peter addresses this same topic in I Peter 4:12-14 to which he says, "Beloved, do not be surprised at the fiery ordeal among you, which comes upon you for your testing, as though some strange thing were happening to you; but to the degree that you share the sufferings of Christ, keep on rejoicing, so that also at the revelation of His glory you may rejoice with exultation. If you are reviled for the name of Christ, you are blessed, because the Spirit of glory and of God rests on you." I love how Peter words that we "share in the sufferings of Christ." As much as we may not like it during the trial, it is an honor that God would allow something bad in our life so that we can relate to what Jesus did for us on the cross. God wants us to experience some of what Christ endured because it gives us empathy and compassion for His sacrifice. If we can relate to Jesus in that way just a little bit it helps give us understanding of how much God loves us.

This may sound obvious, but doing something that scares you is scary! I always revisit this verse whenever I start letting fear get in my own way, "For I am the Lord your God who holds your right hand, and who says to you, 'Do not be afraid. I will help you.'" Isaiah 41:13.

CHAPTER 13

HOPE

"Make this your common practice: Confess your sins to each other and pray for each other so that you can live together whole and healed. The prayer of a person living right with God is something powerful to be reckoned with."

James 5:16 (MSG)

It's impossible to have a personal, intimate relationship with God in just one hour on Sunday. I needed to spend more time with God in fellowship with other people who could relate with me. I also had a lot of questions that were unanswered during church service. I couldn't just stop the pastor and ask him questions that pertain only to me in the middle of his sermon. I felt alone in my recovery. But, I also thought maybe other people were just as afraid to come forward like myself. I couldn't be the only one hurting, suffering, and struggling with habits or addictions in our whole church. So, I thought why not have a recovery support group on Friday nights for a couple of hours? I chose Friday because that can be a tough night for a lot of us who used to go out and party for the weekend. I also wanted to have this group at the church. I knew that no one at the church was working and we wouldn't bother anyone.

On October 23, 2009 I did something completely uncomfortable which freaked me out. God told me to put Christ back into recovery so I started Hope Recovery Small Group. This meant I had to read out loud, pray out loud, and speak in front of people on a weekly basis.

I wanted this group to be inviting to everyone with hurts, habits or addictions. In the past I'd visited recovery meetings where members struggling with the same addictions met together privately. I felt God calling me to do something different, so instead we met as a group, stayed together as a group, and learned together as a group. Even though we had our separate issues, every one of us had emotional scars which left us needing a sense of community where we could feel loved and accepted and share our hurts, habits and addictions without feeling judged. We knew if we put God in the center of our lives, everything else would come together.

Over the next few months I made a commitment to God, my wife and myself that I would make Hope Recovery Small Group on Friday nights a non-negotiable. I would not miss a meeting no matter what. I knew I had to have radical obedience. This was another new habit I was doing to put in place of an unhealthy one. I wanted change so badly. I was totally dependent on God.

The first month of Hope Recovery Small Group was really hard. God began testing me, just like He promised He would. It was only the second Friday night and one of my leaders attacked me pretty bad. She emailed me that night after our meeting and stated she didn't agree with all the things I was planning, and didn't like the direction I was going with Hope. There were so many things in this email that she opposed. The bottom line she was trying to get across to me was that it wasn't all about me. I was so hurt and confused. All I wanted to do was help people and help myself. My gosh, it was only the second night of the small group. I couldn't understand how she was able to say these things to me. I thought she was crazy. I was mad and wrote her back immediately, but I didn't send it right away. I knew I'd better wait so I prayed on it and asked for wise counsel. A couple days had passed and I did the opposite of what I should've done. I sent the email. I soon found out what a big mistake that was. She responded and the emails kept coming one after another. What did I do? I opened a can of worms, and obviously failed God's test. Eventually I stopped responding to her emails and really spent some time with God in prayer. He revealed to me that there was some truth to what the leader was saying. I re-evaluated the whole Friday night Hope Recovery Small Group, and made some changes.

I went through many emotions over the next few weeks. Some of the thoughts that rang through my head were Who am I? What do I know about God? What do I know about recovery? My thoughts were totally correct, I didn't know anything, but that was okay. God let me know that wasn't important, because He had all the answers if I just trusted Him. On Fridays, I was spending about 10 hours preparing and planning out exactly what was going to happen that evening. God told me to not overly plan for Hope Recovery. He told me all He wanted me to do was put chairs in a circle. He also revealed to me that it wasn't about anyone in particular and there didn't have to be a leader in the front of the room teaching. All I have to do is put Him in the center of the circle, then everything else would fall into place. It was so simple, and so hard to do, but from that Friday night until today that's exactly what we do.

It is okay to make mistakes. We may not always do things correctly and may fail the test God gives us. Sometimes we do nothing because we are afraid to fail or be rejected, but if we don't try and move forward, things will never change. During that situation, I was able to learn a lot about myself. My old self would have allowed this setback to mess with my head and possibly even tempt me to go back to my old, destructive ways and attitudes.

Thankfully I was able to reflect and grow, and run the meetings better.

Hope Recovery Small Group has been going strong since then. We never grew to the numbers I was anticipating, but God always shows up on Friday nights in a big way and invites exactly who needs to be there; no matter if it was a couple of us or thirty of us. I believe God kept us small for many reasons. The number one reason I believe was that I wasn't ready. 2 Peter 3:9 says, "God isn't late with his promise as some measure lateness. He is restraining himself on account of you, holding back the End because he doesn't want anyone lost. He's giving everyone space and time to change." God only gives you what you can handle. He also says in Luke 16:10, "If you are faithful in little things, you will be faithful in large ones. But if you are dishonest in little things, you won't be honest with greater responsibilities." Could you imagine if God answered my prayers and forty or fifty people showed up the first couple nights of Hope? What a train wreck that would have been! God taught me early on, that if I was faithful with a small amount, He would trust me with a lot more.

CHAPTER 14

THE NEXT CHAPTER

"What happened in your past is not nearly as important as what is in your future."

- Tony Campolo

Rev. **Billy Graham** tells a time early in his ministry when he arrived in a small town to preach a sermon. Wanting to mail a letter, he asked a young boy where the post office was. When the boy had told him, Dr. Graham thanked him and said, "If you'll come to the Baptist Church this evening, you can hear me telling everyone how to get to heaven." "I don't think I'll be there," the boy said. "You don't even know your way to the post office."

What this little boy said to Rev. Billy Graham was how I felt for most of my life. I had no idea where I was going and I sure didn't know how I was going to get there. Over the years of me growing up, I allowed my circumstances to decide my future. I believed whatever happened to me was it for me. I needed to make the best of my situation, even though something deep down was telling me otherwise.

There was a time in my life where I found myself working at a drug store, at the age of twenty, recently married, with a young daughter. I knew I had to do something bigger, something better than what I was doing at the time. I searched the want ads on my lunch breaks, looked into college and even considered moving. The only answer I could come up with was I needed to make the most of my situation I created for myself, and I should be grateful I had a job. I was settling for what I thought I deserved, but God wants so much more for our lives.

In Jeremiah 29:11, it says, "'For I know the plans I have for you,' declares the Lord. 'They are plans for good and not for disaster, to give you a future and a hope.'" What this verse says to me is my God cares enough and loves me enough to make plans way in advance for me. These plans aren't average either because my God is not average, my God is huge! He wants the absolute best for me. He wants me to have a hope and purpose in life, bigger than myself. He doesn't want my circumstances to decide my future. Once I realized this and started living it out, I knew that nothing could ever stop me from allowing God's purpose in my life.

I was spending my Sundays directing the children's department at my church's second location, and I was loving every second of it. I was also still leading the Hope Recovery Small Group and enjoying my time there as well. I even finished up my schooling and became a certified pastor.

The opportunity to be the children's director for all campuses came my way after the previous director left. I had mixed feelings about applying for the position. I didn't want to be locked into a career and felt God pulling me in a different direction. I wasn't sure what direction yet, but it was leading me away from children's ministry. I talked about taking the lead position with my wife and she encouraged me to ask the senior pastor if I was even a candidate for the position. I would have benefits, retirement, and a steady paycheck, after all. My wife and I were just getting settled into our new home with our blended families, and this job would help us feel more stable. Having this position was a safe choice for me.

She brought up some very good points so I emailed the senior pastor the next day. I just wanted to know if I was even being considered for the position. He emailed me back that same day and his answer surprised me. He said no. A small part of me wanted him to say yes so that I could at least have the option of turning him down. My ego was shot. He told me that they were looking for an experienced children's pastor, a "superstar" to take the church to the next level, and I wasn't it. At the time, I was really disappointed. Sometimes we think we know what's best for us and we pray and pray for it to happen. Sometimes it does happen and sometimes it does not. God's ways are not our ways. He can see the whole path of where He wants us, but we can only see what is right in front of us. What I should've done is said so clearly in this verse:

"So we fix our eyes not on what is seen, but on what is unseen. For what is seen is temporary, but what is unseen is eternal." 2 Corinthians 4:18. God always answers our prayers. He doesn't always do it in the way we want him to, but He'll always answer with one of the following: "Yes", "No, I have something better for you", or "Wait". I am so thankful that God didn't answer all my prayers with a "Yes." As I reflect back, God told the pastor to reject me for the position because He had something better planned for me.

I decided after that to pour more of my attention into Hope Recovery Small Group. It wasn't that long before I knew I had to step away from what I was currently doing in the children's department completely. I was spending more and more time planning the small groups that I was not devoting enough time to the children. They deserved 100% of my time, and I wasn't able to give that to them. I felt like I was cheating them. It broke my heart to say goodbye, but I had a peace about it because I know sometimes you have to say no to good in order to do great.

The poem below demonstrates why God says no to some of our prayers. Many think that when God says no to a prayer, that must mean He didn't hear our prayer or doesn't care about us. But it's the exact opposite; sometimes He answers us with a no because He has something better in mind, or wants us to learn a valuable lesson.

Most Richly Blessed

I asked God for strength, that I might achieve,
I was made weak, that I might learn humbly to obey
I asked for health, that I might do greater things,
I was given infirmity, that I might do better things
I asked for riches, that I might be happy,
I was given poverty, that I might be wise.
I asked for power, that I might have praise of men,
I was given weakness, that I might feel the need of God.
I asked for all things, that I might enjoy all things.
I got nothing I asked for –
But everything I had hoped for,
Almost despite myself, my
Unspoken prayers were answered.
I am, among all men,
Most richly blessed.

One Friday night a young kid and his father showed up at Hope Recovery Small Group. The father explained to me how his son was struggling with drugs and he was in and out of trouble since the age of 13., He was now 24 years old. For the sake of the person's To protect his identity we will call the young kid "Johnny."

Johnny never had a job and was the father of a young child himself. He was living at home with his parents, and his mother and father were at their wits' end. The father had no idea what to do for Johnny.

The first night Johnny and his father showed up at Hope Recovery, Johnny just sat there and listened. He really didn't say much. I could tell he liked the group, though. My wife and I instantly fell in love with this kid and wanted to help him anyway we knew how. The next few Friday nights Johnny came back and was really opening up more and began to grow as a person. My wife and I knew he was getting something out of this group. The only negative thing Johnny shared with me was that he wished the group met more often. Hope only met once a week for about an hour and a half. He wanted more, and it got me thinking about how we could give him more.

The following Friday Johnny didn't show up. My wife and I texted him and called him, but got no response. Another Friday went by and still no Johnny. The next Sunday I ran into his dad. He explained to me how the police came in the middle of the night and arrested Johnny. He was doing drugs and running amuck during the week and it finally caught up with him. My heart broke for him. Maybe if we offered the small group more nights a week or even had a place for people to go during the week, we could have saved him. It was right at that moment that God spoke to me and told me to open up a recovery center.

The next few months I started doing a ton of research. The first alarming thing I discovered was that there were no faith-based recovery centers around. I looked in the phone book and found some that were located a few cities away. The ones I found were so expensive I wondered how anyone could afford to get help. I was able to find a couple in-patient facilities for a low cost, but the length of the programs were a year or longer. Those programs are great, but just not for everyone. God was really telling me we needed more faith-based recovery centers.

I began my quest with researching all the rehabilitation centers in a hundred mile radius from me. I called center and after center to ask about prices, their program and everything they had to offer. After all my research was finished, I looked at my notes and realized that what I was looking for didn't exist. I was left with two options. I could go on living my life knowing that someone should start some kind of recovery facility that was centered around God, or I would have to do it myself.

I was so passionate about starting a recovery center I shared my dream with everyone I talked to. One day two good friends of mine asked me what it would take for me to get it started. I knew I needed to hire a lawyer and that would cost me $5000 dollars. A few days later at church, these friends presented me with a check for that same amount. I remember one of the friends looked me in the eye and said to me, "I'm not giving this money to you, I'm giving it to God. Because if I was giving it to you, I wouldn't give you a dime." I'm so glad that he was specific with where he intended the money to go, and he was right to let me know it. He was another reminder to me that we should put our trust in God, and not in other people.

When meeting with a lawyer I was able to haggle over the price he had given me and saved myself $1000, which I was able to use later for a website. A week after meeting with my lawyer he filed the Articles of Incorporation with the state of California and on August 31, 2010 Hope Recovery Center Inc. was born.

So now what? We were incorporated, had a website and filed for a non-profit 501(c)(3). I put my trust in God and he guided me and brought people in my life I needed to succeed in this scary endeavor. I started a board of directors, and we began meeting weekly to pray about the future of Hope Recovery Center Inc. My board of directors were from all different kinds of walks: we had a stay at home mom who was a fundraising guru, one was a scientist, another was an analyst, we had a former drug addict who runs two successful construction businesses and another who is a nanny for a very popular rock band. They all brought their God-given talent to the table and were able to use their talents to help get the center pointed in the right direction. Looking back, who would ever thought we could open up a recovery center. No one had any experience running one, and it was going to be run by an alcoholic, drug addicted, former children's pastor. Sometimes it seems that God is crazy bringing all of us together with our different backgrounds, but I firmly believe in the Bible verse that says, "With God all things are possible" (Mark 10:27).

I carry a coin around with me everywhere I go, and it has this Bible verse on it. I found this coin at a Christian book store. There was a container filled with coins on a display counter and I casually picked up a few and started reading what was on them. One had a picture of Mary, another one had the Christian symbol of a fish, but then I saw one that had a cross on one side, and Mark 10:27 on the other. I was immediately drawn to the last coin. I was in the midst of battling self-doubt about how I could even possibly run a recovery center, and this Bible verse had the answer I needed to reaffirm that I would be successful because with God all things are possible.

I carry this coin around with me everywhere I go. I keep it in the same pocket as my vial of nitroglycerin. This medicine is in case I were to have chest pains or possibly another heart attack or cardiac arrest. When I walk, the coin constantly clinks against the vial and is a constant reminder that anything is possible as long as I put God in the center of my life. I hear the jingling in my pocket and it's almost like God is whispering in my ear, "Quit questioning me and keep trusting me."

I wanted each of my board members to have this same coin. I found them online and bought a handful to pass out to them at our next board meeting. Now, every board meeting we have is centered around the theme "With God all things are possible." We kept praying for God to guide us and on May 2, 2011 we opened Hope Recovery Center Inc. with only enough money to open the doors. We didn't know how we were going to pay next month's expenses, but we knew that God was involved and anything was possible. Even to this day, we still don't know how we are going to pay for the following month, but God always provides.

Remember how I wrote about the fact that just because you become a Christian doesn't mean your life won't have any difficulties? Within the first year of opening Hope Recovery Center Inc. we experienced helping a woman save her baby from abortion and give it up for adoption, alcoholism, drug addiction, cutting, depression, attempted suicide, missing persons, bipolar disorder, schizophrenia, 5150 holds at hospitals, domestic violence, child abuse, child custody issues, homelessness, Asperger's, grand mal seizures, pedophilia, theft, restraining order, divorce, prison, jail, prostitution, drug overdose and frequent visits from parole officers and probation officers. In its first year of opening, Hope Recovery Center Inc. became more than a rehabilitation center for addicts. Because of the challenges God sent our way, Hope is a center for anyone struggling with hurts, habits or addictions.

CHAPTER 15

SECOND CHANCES

"I don't know what the day holds,
but I know Who holds the day."

I **want to** challenge you to do something new today. Change your thinking for just a bit and take the focus off yourself. Take the focus off of the pain and struggles you're dealing with today. I know it's hard, but remember, you're trying something new.

What if you could have a second chance? What if it might be a third, fourth, or even thirtieth time to get it right? There's always a chance for a new beginning, but you have to be willing to take that first step.

I wrote about believing in God and how important it is to have faith that He can do a miracle in your life. But believing God exists isn't enough to get you out of your storm; even Satan believes in God (James 2:19). So what's the next step? The next step is taking action. The Bible says in James: 2:15-24, "Dear friends, do you think you'll get anywhere in this if you learn all the right words but never do anything? Does merely talking about faith indicate that a person really has it? For instance, you come upon an old friend dressed in rags and half-starved and say, 'Good morning, friend! Be clothed in Christ! Be filled with the Holy Spirit!' and walk off without providing so much as a coat or a cup of soup—where does that get you? Isn't it obvious that God-talk without God-acts is outrageous nonsense? I can already hear one of you agreeing by saying, 'Sounds good. You take care of the faith department, I'll handle the works department.' Not so fast. You can no more show me your works apart from your faith than I can show you my faith apart from my works. Faith and works, works and faith, fit together hand in glove. Do I hear you professing to believe in the one and only God, but then observe you complacently sitting back as if you had done something wonderful? That's just great. Demons do that, but what good does it do them? Use your heads! Do you suppose for a minute that you can cut faith and works in two and not end up with a corpse on your hands? Wasn't our ancestor Abraham 'made right with God by works when he placed his son Isaac on the sacrificial altar? Isn't it obvious that faith and works are yoked partners, that faith expresses itself in works? That the works are 'works of faith'? The full meaning of 'believe' in the Scripture sentence, 'Abraham believed God and was set right with God,' includes his action. It's that mesh of believing and acting that got Abraham named 'God's friend.' Is it not evident that a person is made right with God not by a barren faith but by faith fruitful in works?"

I love this description in the Message Bible. In the book of James, James makes a compelling comparison to Abraham from the Old Testament. God told Abraham to sacrifice his own son for the testing of his faith. God wanted to see if Abraham would be obedient to Him and sacrifice his own son as a burnt offering. Abraham agreed and took his son to the place where he would be sacrificed. Right before Abraham drew his knife to kill his own son, God stopped him and provided a ram to take the place of his son.

Abraham showed such radical obedience to God that he was willing to kill his own son to show how obedient he was. God isn't asking us to do this today, but he does want to see radical obedience like Abraham showed. He wants us to take action and not just say we have faith. Show it. Abraham trusted God to guide him, even if it meant losing his own son. Luckily for Abraham, God provided the animal instead.

What do you need to sacrifice in your life? What do you need to get rid of? Are you addicted? What pain are you holding onto that you won't let go of? What are you not trusting God with? I mentioned before that we were going to try something new today. It's scary, but that's ok. Try taking whatever is holding you back from the life God wants you to have and give it to Him. Surrender all the pain, addiction, hurts, habits, etc. and allow God to deal with it so you don't have to. Take action.

Regardless of where you have been God wants to fulfill His promises He has for you, if you will receive them, (Jeremiah 29:11-13) This is a gift. This is a choice. It is not easy all the time, but I bet your life has not always been easy. I promise, however, that it is worth it. I experience now and know the unconditional love, acceptance, and forgiveness from God alone. It is always a choice. I ask you to look at yourself and realize you are here on this earth for special meaning and purpose. Find the joy, peace, love and hope, only He can give you, by seeking Him. Give Him a try, put Him to the test. In my life I have lost everything that I thought I had, to find out who I really am...I am His, a child of God. That can't take to any title, job, car, or material thing I have had or felt to make me complete. Pour your heart and soul into God, lean on Him for everything. Give Him your hurt, your brokenness, your fears, your heart. He will lift you up like it says in Isaiah 41:10, "Do not fear, for I am with you. Do not be afraid, for I am God. I will give you strength, and for sure I will help you. Yes, I will hold you up with my right hand that is right and good."

If you are tired of living the crazy cycle of addiction, bondage, heartache or pain from this life, give yourself completely to Him. Put God in the center of your life and watch everything come together. Seek Him, and He will do the rest. Give up the control and surrender. There is nothing better than that. We try to complicate things so much and make them harder than it needs to be. Keep it simple. Put Him first, and He will make miracles out of our messes.

I always felt there was something else for me, but I didn't know how to get it. I lost a lot of years by doing things my way. I have also learned so much in the process. I live with no more regrets because it is making me the person I am becoming. I can't change the past, but I can determine my direction. If I fully rely on God, I am confident in my future. I no longer look at things as bad and question, "how could this be happening?", but I look at what can I learn from the situation. I choose to respond and not react when things go wrong. I see obstacles now as opportunities to grow. I may not do it exactly right, but I am learning all the time.

AFTERWARD

The Serenity Prayer

*God grant me the serenity
to accept the things I cannot change;
courage to change the things I can;
and wisdom to know the difference.*

Many addicts recite the Serenity Prayer to help guide them in their recovery. When I first found this prayer I liked it, and it made sense, but I never made a personal connection with it. So during my recovery I created my own prayer that was specific to my life and the goals I set for myself. It is the essence of my purpose.

My Primary Aim

My Primary Aim is all about having an intimate, close relationship with God, my wife and kids.

It's about being generous, being a man of character, being healthy and being real.

Each day I strive to live my life on purpose for the Lord.

LETTERS FROM FRIENDS

I have included several stories from individuals who are part of our Hope Family and/or have successfully completed our program at Hope Recovery Center Inc.

BAD THINGS HAPPEN TO GOOD PEOPLE

By: Stacy Dorsey

Hope is not only there for addictions but also for the emotional and physical hurts as well. Being an over-comer of sexual abuse since the age of 6 I understand the emotional trauma a person goes through. While the scars may no longer be on your skin the internal scars, though years old, can feel like only yesterday. The memories can haunt your dreams and the baggage affects your every relationship.

I was raised in a Christian home with loving parents and a wonderful support group who loved and adored me. Yet at the hands of a demented boy my six year old body was violated and my sacred most intimate gift was ripped from me. Too ashamed and scared I never told my parents, or anyone. I lived with the memory and devastation allowing it to determine my self-worth.

How can a loving God allow such pain and hurt and injustice on a child? I asked myself that question time and time again. While relationship after relationship ended I felt myself drowning in a sea of abandonment, abuse, neglect and overwhelming self-hatred. The fear of rejection became paralyzing for me. While on the outside I appeared to be bubbly, outgoing and confident on the inside I was that little girl looking for approval and only finding pain. So pain became my approval, it seemed normal to accept abuse and infidelity in my relationships. After all I wasn't worth anything else, right?

It wasn't until I met my husband, Jon, in 2006 that I began to see myself the way God saw me. It had always been easy to pray for others but why would God want to hear my cry for help? After all I wore a scarlet letter after more than four decades of allowing men to use me as an object. Jon saw me differently; he saw the Jesus in me. He prayed with me, comforted me and I was finally able to see the God who cried with me the day my innocence was stolen. The Jesus who held me up when I could no longer stand the pain any longer, the Holy Spirit who whispered in my ear, "I am with you" when I felt more alone then I could bear. The very thing that broke me, a man, was the thing God used to start the healing process.

My name is Stacy Dorsey and I am the Counseling Director at Hope Recovery. It amazes me how God can use someone like me, to heal the broken-hearted. I thank Him daily for the opportunity to be a part of Hope Recovery. I pray that God will continue to bless the efforts of the broken as we step out on faith and do his will.

"You intended to harm me, but God intended it for good to accomplish what is now being done, the saving of many lives."

-Genesis 50:20

G O D   U S E S   B R O K E N   P E O P L E

By: Nicole Michelle Willin

Let me first paint a picture for you of who I once was. I went through seasons of destruction and different types of destructive behaviors.

I reached a point where I had lost everything, including my children. I went from living in my own home to moving in with a man who was involved in an outlaw biker gang. I saw things most people couldn't even imagine. So I learned to shut off my emotions and just not feel. The moment he told me he loved me out the door I went. I didn't love myself so how could anybody else. I continued with this pattern with a few more men along the way.

My drug use and drinking progressed. I couldn't find a stable place to live and began hanging out with a man who is now serving a Life Sentence. I was actually a codefendant and part of that case. This was the first time I went to jail. I was facing 5 ½ years in prison. You would think that would've slowed me down, but actually my life continued to get worse.

I was out on bail, and I missed a court date. This was a high-profile case so immediately the bounty hunters began looking for me. For months they were on my tail. There was even an award out for my capture. I wouldn't stay at any one place very long, knowing they were right behind me.

Eventually they found me. I was with a friend, and we went on a high speed chase with the bounty hunters, until we turned a corner and there were police everywhere with spike strips in the streets. They stopped us at gun point. The police pulled me from the truck, had me on my knees, hands on my head, the whole nine yards. They took me to jail for 5 months this time. I continued down this scary and devastating road and found myself in jail time and time again. I never once thought of my consequences.

At one point I was kidnapped by a man. He was a codefendant on yet another case. He was under the impression that I would "rat" him out. He held a knife to my throat, threatening me. I wasn't even scared. I looked at him and told him to "go ahead, and stick it in". I believe he was so taken back by my lack of fear he let me go.

I would've rather somebody else take my life, so that the heartache and devastation I was causing my family and children would end. What a warped way of rationalizing my actions.

The morning I was arrested for the last time, one of my co-defendants and I had made a plan. Her ex-husband is an Indian. His family owns a casino. We were planning on driving out to the casino that morning. She was going to sleep with him while I robbed him. The thing about this that is most disturbing to me now, is the fact that we knew, if we were to go through with this, eventually his tribe would hunt us down, torture us, and probably chop us up and bury us on the Reservation. Once again I had no regard for my life.

Well God works in mysterious ways... On our way out of town that morning we were pulled over in a stolen car. I knew I was facing a prison term.

In the midst of all my jail visits I had become friends with a Bail Bondsman. He came to visit me the night before I had court. He told me "do not sign for your prison term" he was going to bail me out by midnight the next night. I thought this was a great idea. I could fight this case from the streets. I went back to my cell that night after our visit, and God spoke to me. God said, "Be still". Little did I know that's actually a verse in the Bible. "Be still and know that I am God." (Psalm 46:10) . I sat and thought about this and I knew that I could come out of this one of two ways, the same woman that I came in as or a as a new creation.

I went to court that next morning and took a plea, I signed for a prison term. I felt at peace; I was done fighting the battle. I remember calling my mom and telling her that I was going to prison. We both cried. But my tears weren't tears of heartache, this time they were tears of relief.

While I served my time I couldn't get enough of God's word. I read my Bible every chance I had. I attended church services and Bible studies. Before I paroled I told my mom that I needed a church and some sort of recovery group. She went online and the first thing she found was the Hope Recovery Small Group. I paroled on a Thursday and that very next night I attended the Hope Recovery Small Group. Talk about scary, walking into the lobby of a church one day out of prison. I had to remind myself that I wasn't leading anymore, I was following God. I haven't missed a Hope Friday night since. September 9th will mark the two year anniversary that I've been out of prison.

That very same weekend that I paroled I began attending church. My dad went to church with me as well. A man who didn't go to church is now serving every weekend and has a beautiful relationship with God. Two weeks after I paroled I began serving in the children's ministry, thanks to the nudge of Shawn and Stacey. One month after my parole date Shawn got me driving the church truck every Sunday for the satellite church. I did this for ten months. Within nine months of my parole I've gotten my license back, bought a car, and regained custody of my children.

My relationship with my family and kids was being transformed day by day. And I now cherish them. My mom told me recently that "I am one of God's Frontline Soldiers." I know that I am and that I will remain one. I went from just surviving each day, not having any thirst for life to basking in every breath I take. I have nobody to thank but God, but I also don't know where I would be without my family, without Hope Recovery, and my Hope family.

Thank you for reading the story God has given me. My name is Nicole Michelle Willin and I am the Assistant Director at Hope Recovery Center.

"He will cover you with his feathers. He will shelter you with his wings. His faithful promises are your armor and protection."

- Psalm 91:4

MY SPIRITUAL HOME

By: Clarence White, Jr.

Hope is my spiritual home. I came here a little lost. I have learned to be more accepting and loving to others. I've become, I hope, a better parent. Hope has given me more patience. I've learned that we're all a little weird, in our special ways. And that it is OK. Hope has shown me that I was selfish in my old ways. For me it is a special place that I can come and be who I am, and not feel judged by others. It's a place that I've made many new friends. I've found out that I'm not alone in this, that there are many others like me. Hope has reminded me that it is noble to serve. Hope has allowed me to bless others by the things I've been through. My hope is that I share something that saves another in truly finding themselves. Hope has helped me find ME.

God bless and take care.

WHAT HOPE RECOVERY MEANS TO ME

By: Michele Zamora

Hope Recovery Center Inc. means hope, faith, and love. I first started going to Hope in July of 2011. I met Pastor Shawn and Stacey Kelly at a Bible study they had at a sober living apartment complex I was in. I didn't understand anything they were talking about and was too afraid to ask. After the study, Pastor Shawn told me about Hope Recovery Small Group they have every Friday night. I decided to go because I needed something other than AA meetings. When I got there I noticed everyone had Bibles but me. I had never read one. I was praying that they wouldn't pick me to read because I didn't know where to turn to in my Bible. That's one of the awesome things that Hope has taught me. I've gone through the program, graduated, 120 days with honors. I am still learning about myself with the help of an on-site therapist, counseling, and my best friend. This program has helped me deal with my emotions without having to cut, use, or drink. I know now that I was never alone, God was always right there waiting for me to ask for Him to help me. The people at Hope Recovery Center Inc are the most loving, caring, giving, people I've ever met. They have shown and taught me so much in the year I've been here now that I now teach Bible study, have small groups, show clients how to open their Bibles, let them know I didn't know how to either, volunteer, and be of service. They've showed me how to be affectionate; I love to give hugs now. That's my way of giving encouragement. Hope has truly changed my life and the ways I live it. I now live by God's will, not mine, I accepted Jesus Christ as my Lord and Savior in August 2011 and was baptized by Pastor Shawn. It was amazing. I like to say I was born and raised at Hope Recovery Center Inc.

With God all things are possible!

HOW HOPE HAS BEEN AN INFLUENCE ON MY LIFE

By: Tammy Shelton

A friend brought me to church one Saturday evening and Shawn Kelly was giving his testimony. Something in his testimony caught me. At this time I did not attend church nor did I ever have a relationship with God. My life was broken, failed marriage and full of depression. Shawn mentioned the Hope Center was for people with hurts, habits and/or addictions. I went to the first Wednesday meeting not sure what to expect. I found a room full of loving, caring, honest & faithful people. Shortly after that I started attending Friday night Bible Study.

The staff and volunteers at Hope accepted me broken and I now have my Hope family which is full of love, hope and friendship. Hope counsels the broken, and teaches faith, love, hope, life skills, how to give back to your community, how to have a relationship with God and that with God all things are possible. I wish I was able to attend the classes during the day.

Today my depression is under control, I am learning to put God in the center of my life. I have the tools to help myself get through life's trials and know that these trials are normal and there will always be lessons and growth to be learned from them. I now have a relationship with God! I owe this to Shawn, Stacey, Stacy, Nicole and everyone else who has come through the center.

MY HOPE FAMILY

By: Kristen Moreno

I came to Hope small group angry and full of self-hatred but what I found was family and the beginnings of understanding unconditional love. I have always struggled with admitting my lifelong addiction to alcohol and drugs because I had always been a functioning addict so seeking help was not an option. I knew that God and church attendance would be a good and safe starting place for me but it wasn't enough because I wasn't developing relationships so I kept drinking.

After about a month of getting involved with Hope I knew I was all in and totally invested in the ministry. Not only was I able to begin to make human connections but I began to experience a relationship with Jesus Christ. This faith community embraced me, included my family and me, stepped up to help when it was needed, and most importantly provided spiritual guidance. Almost two years in and I do not miss any weeks. They are my family and who I am doing life with. I am no longer ashamed of my addictions because God has a future and a hope for me that He developed especially for the person that He created me to be. I no longer feel lost or like I don't belong. I am learning to love myself and to accept the love of others especially, God. Today I have been clean and sober for almost two years. In the last 20+ years this is the longest I have ever made it and I owe it all to my Lord and Savior and my Hope family.

A LETTER TO MY SOULMATE

By: Stacey Kelly

Since Shawn and I were brought together, it has been an adventure/journey. Although our hearts met and we were joined quickly, I realize now that I didn't have a clue what was in store for us. From the beginning, Shawn shared his heart, passions, and dreams with me. We were very transparent and honest about where we had been and where we wanted to go in our new lives.

Through my struggles and dark times, I always had that small voice inside telling me that I would be okay. Jeremiah 29:11 was what I held on to when I didn't know what to do or what the future would hold. Someone once said to me, "what's holding you back?" I knew I had allowed my situation and circumstances around me to hold me down in fear and self doubt. However, when I recommitted my life to God, I wanted to no longer live a life of regrets. I didn't want to look back at the past but instead look toward what could be in my future. So when I met Shawn, I knew it was just the beginning.

Initially, I had a slight hesitation about getting involved with an addict/alcoholic. I had grown up in an alcoholic home and knew how it affected friends and family around me. I didn't want to go from one bad situation to another, but I was quickly reassured when seeing Shawn's focus, heart, and determination to serve God in his new life with a new direction. I remember when he shared about his dream of opening a recovery center in the future- which I was sure was a 5-year plan! Little did I know, we would begin Hope Recovery Small Group after dating only 2 months and open Hope Recovery Center after 1 year, 3 months of marriage! It is crazy and amazing to see how we "think" we know the plan for our lives. However, when we truly commit and surrender ourselves and our plans to God, we are in for a journey /adventure that can be far more than we ever dreamed possible.

When Shawn used to share with me his ideas, plans, and goals, I would agree and say, "we will pray about it and see." Incredibly, whenever we did, God showed up. Shawn often challenged me when I might question things happening by saying, "My God is Big; how big is your God?" I would get so mad initially, but I don't question it anymore. Now I know better. If Shawn says he is going to do something, I don't doubt it. If he writes it down and speaks it out, I know we better be ready. When we trust God, He does show up. Not only does He show up, but He does it huge! His plans are far better and different than we think or plan.

We have had so many times when we didn't have the resources or qualifications to accomplish the tasks in front of us, but we have been blessed to have people and things happen to complete all of them. We agreed to walk in faith and radical obedience with our marriage, family, and Hope Recovery Ministries, and we haven't been let down since. By far, it has not always been easy. At times, it has been scary, but He has always met our needs. Every month, we come up short to pay the bills, and yet we are still open and growing. We always say, God is never early, but He is always on time.

It is not always easy being married to an addict who wants everything now and struggles with his old self and old ways. However, I know God is leading him every step even when he can't see what's ahead. Also, I know God brought us together for a purpose. Lastly, I know all things will work together for good because... With God all things are possible. I am confident in God's promises because I have seen them and experienced them. It is not always about getting the rewards, but it is about the process and what we learn along the way. I am so thankful for my new life with Shawn, getting the opportunity to be part of Hope Recovery, and living a life that I could have never imagined until now.

HOPE
Recovery Center, Inc.

OUT-PATIENT RECOVERY PROGRAM

Hope Recovery Center Inc., provides a FREE customized, faith based, outpatient treatment program for hurts, habits and addictions. Our Extended Care gives each client the opportunity to build a strong foundation of recovery while living at home in their own environment with the guidance of our professional staff.

Our treatment program is down-to-earth and faith-centered. Christ is the center focus of our group therapy and individualized sessions help us understand the needs of each client, who must accept their need and then take responsibility for the life God has given them for the process of recovery.

Hope Recovery Center understands how important each life is to God and the community, and that is why we insist on being non-profit.

- ○ Relationship Counseling
- ○ Marriage Counseling
- ○ Parenting
- ○ Communication
- ○ Grief
- ○ Fear
- ○ Resentment
- ○ Childhood Trauma
- ○ Anxiety

- ○ Abandonment Loneliness
- ○ Self-Esteem
- ○ Anger Management
- ○ Guilt
- ○ Depression
- ○ Panic Attacks
- ○ Co-Dependency
- ○ Life Change

Hope Recovery Center, Inc.

9036 Pulsar Court, Ste. H, Corona, CA 92883

(951) 603-0031 / info@hoperecoverycenterinc.org

www.HopeRecoveryCenterInc.org

$10 CHALLENGE

Hope Recovery Center, Inc. needs you to open your hearts to hope and partner with us with our brand new $10 Challenge! Together, we can make a difference in someone's life by committing to donate $10 per month and telling 10 other people to do the same.

The Facts:

- *1 in 3 people in your immediate family have struggled with addition.*

- *The success rated with completing a secular recovery program is 2-5% versus that of a faith-based recovery program which is an amazing 80%!*

- *Hope Recovery Center, Inc. offers custom treatment plans which include individual and group counseling by trained professionals. Our classes also include psychology, spiritual, academic, and vocational training in a safe and encouraging environment.*

Your commitment of only $10 per month can change lives by giving hope and purpose to those who are broken and lost.

Hope Recovery Center, Inc.
9036 Pulsar Ct. Ste H
Corona, Ca. 92883
(951) 603-0031
www.HopeRecoveryCenterInc.org